MW01027114

I Remember
JIM VALVANO

I Remember
JIM VALVANO

*Personal Reflections and Anecdotes about College
Basketball's Most Exuberant Final Four Coach,
as Told by the People and Players Who Knew Him*

MIKE TOWLE

**Cumberland House
Nashville, Tennessee**

Copyright © 2001 by Michael J. Towle

A portion of the author's royalties are being donated to the
V Foundation.

Published by
CUMBERLAND HOUSE PUBLISHING, INC.
431 Harding Industrial Drive
Nashville, TN 37211
www.CumberlandHouse.com

Cover design by Gore Studio, Inc.

Library of Congress Cataloging-in-Publication Data
Towle, Mike.
   I remember Jim Valvano : personal reflections and anecdotes about college basketball's most exuberant final four coach as told by the people and players who knew him / Mike Towle.
      p. cm.
   Includes index.
   ISBN 1-58182-219-7 (alk. paper)
   1. Valvano, Jim. 2. Valvano, Jim—Friends and associates.
3. Basketball coaches—United States—Biography. I. Title.

GV884.V34 T69 2001
796.323'092–dc21
[B]   2001047275

Printed in the United States of America
2 3 4 5 6 7 8 9 10—17 16 15 14 13 12

To Coach V and Terry B

Contents

ACKNOWLEDGMENTS

Putting together a work likes this requires a lot of cooperation from a lot of people. A heartfelt thanks go to the following:

Pam Valvano, Jim's widow, not only made herself accessible for this book, she opened up in recalling insightful and personal details from her life with one of college basketball's most exciting, exuberant, and at times exasperating coaches. Pam and her daughter LeeAnn were also instrumental in arranging access to numerous other people interviewed for this book.

Nick Valvano, Jim's older brother, carved out a sizable chunk of one very hectic afternoon to make time to provide memories of his brother. Joyce Aschenbrenner, Frank McCann, and everyone else at the V Foundation stepped in and provided assistance along the way, and they did it cheerfully.

Annabelle Vaughan, Brian Reinhardt, and the N.C. State athletic media relations office were most accommodating in providing research materials and granting access to the reams of Jimmy V clip files that provided much-needed background for this book. Also helping out in the area of collegiate sports information were Tim Bourrett at Clemson and the folks at Rutgers, Johns Hopkins, Connecticut, Bucknell, and Iona.

Jimmy V covered a lot of ground during his short lifetime, and all of those people helped in filling in the blanks.

Dozens of people were contacted for interviews and assistance with this book, and most responded, and many of those with enthusiasm. Perhaps even a few friendships were forged in the process. Those pitching in one way or another were Rich Petriccione, Linda Bruno, Jeff Ruland, Bill Foster, Bob Lloyd, Pam Valvano, Nick Valvano, LeeAnn Valvano, Frank McCann, Tom Penders, Dereck Whittenburg, Michael Warren, Terry Gannon, Ray Martin, Pat Kennedy, Jerry Tarkanian, Lefty Driesell, Alexander Wolff, Charles Chandler, Chris Corchiani, Fred Davis, Tommy Thompson, Paul Biko, Kenneth Lambert, Dick Vitale, Billy Packer, Pat Kennedy, Algin Garrett, Max Perry, and Vinny Del Negro.

As always, my wife Holley and son Andrew were patient troupers in turning Dad loose for hours and days on end to work on and finish this project. Our friends at Cornerstone Church in Nashville have been there for us, to include Greg Beatty and the entire parking lot gang. John and Mae Chambers have been faithful stewards with their time and love.

To Jesus Christ, my lord and savior, who is nothing but (safety) net.

PREFACE

My only up-close-and-personal moment involving Jim Valvano took place on an outer concourse that encircles the basketball court at Reunion Arena in Dallas. It was Final Four Saturday in 1986, one week after Valvano's N.C. State Wolfpack had been eliminated from the NCAA Tournament in a Midwest Regional final loss to Kansas.

It was either at halftime of one of that Saturday's semi-finals or between games when I left my seat in the press area and stepped out into the concourse. I wanted to wander about and see who among the hundreds of college coaches in attendance I might run into so I could have an impromptu interview and piece together a nice little sidebar for my paper, the *Fort Worth Star-Telegram*. Every few seconds while strolling through this (Bob) Knight gallery, I would spot a big-name coach either hanging out with family, friends, or fans; buying a hotdog and coke; or simply scurrying—kind of like that black-suited mystery guy carrying the umbrella alongside the JFK motorcade in Dealey Plaza—so as to avoid the many clusters of people positioning themselves for the opportunity to gravitate toward a Mr. Wonderful. This was a basketball junkie's version of taking a charge.

Suddenly, he appeared. Big nose, big grin, no airs. It was Jim Valvano in the flesh, strolling through Reunion Arena; destination, who knows? He could just as well have been coming out of the men's room in search of the lavatory worker who restocks the toilet paper. It didn't matter. Valvano was on the scene and all eyes were on him. He was a basketball coach, sure; but he was more. A celebrity, let's say. A walking, talking sportswriter's dream—a quote machine who geared up for moments like this, as several reporters and numerous other hangers-on quickly jumped in and surrounded Coach V. Responding to questions about some long-since-forgotten front-sports-page issue of the day, Valvano was glib, funny, and charming. Something else, too. How else to describe it?

HE WAS BIGGER THAN LIFE.

That, quite honestly, was what kept going through my mind. This was Jimmy V, and he was bigger than life. I don't know how else to describe it or explain it. It wasn't an optical illusion, and I was suffering from no delusions as far as I know. He appeared to be about six feet, maybe six-one, and about 185 pounds or so; a bit bigger than the average man, but somewhat smallish by basketball standards. There was just something about Valvano hard to put a finger on, except that he could fill a room, or at least what seemed like a good portion of a concourse.

Three years earlier Valvano had won what would be his only national title, but in 1986 he still hadn't written an autobiography, made it onto David Letterman's short-list rotation, done network television basketball, been fired from N.C. State, been diagnosed with cancer, or made his memorable ESPYs speech. This was before Jim Valvano was universally Jimmy V, and he *already* had presence. Big-time presence.

In *I Remember Jim Valvano*, many people from his past tell, in their own words, what they remember about this unforgettable basketball coach out of New York. Along the way, they help explain what it was about Valvano that made him bigger than life.

I Remember

JIM VALVANO

1
I OWN A COLLEGE

It was one of Jim Valvano's favorite lines: "I Own a College." When he was a coach at Iona College in the late seventies, that was his stock response to strangers who queried him about where he coached. Here was a smart-mouthed guy who, in a sense, did own his own college. Valvano spent five seasons at the school in New Rochelle, New York, transforming it from a little-known Eastern Seaboard doormat to one of the top twenty basketball programs in the country, thanks in large part to a big All-American center by the name of Jeff Ruland. Valvano was head basketball coach, athletic director, and—the six-foot-eleven Ruland notwithstanding—big man on campus.

College basketball fans who saw Valvano and his 1983 Cinderella N.C. State Wolfpack as an overnight sensation couldn't have known that this was a guy who had paid his dues, who before coming to N.C. State in 1980 had already spent more than a decade as a college basketball coach, first as an assistant at his alma mater, Rutgers, followed by a one-year stint as head coach at Johns Hopkins, then two years as an assistant at Connecticut, followed by three years as head coach at Bucknell, and then the five years at Iona. Overnight sensation? Hardly.

Valvano was a basketball nut who got the most out of his talent in more ways than one: first as a starting guard at Rutgers for three years alongside All-American and roommate Bob Lloyd, and then as a Wolfpack coach, most conspicuously in 1983, when he led a so-so team of nonstars to the pinnacle of the college hoops world, capped by an unforgettable 54–52 triumph over Houston in the title game in Albuquerque, New Mexico.

Here's a look back at Valvano's pre-Raleigh college years, starting with his playing days at Rutgers in the mid-sixties.

⌁

Bob Lloyd *was one of Valvano's closest friends for the last twenty-five years of V's life. They played basketball together at Rutgers in the sixties as backcourt teammates, and they ended up rooming together. Lloyd, reserved and neat, and Valvano, brash and not as neat, were a real life Felix Unger and Oscar Madison, although it took Lloyd a few days after he arrived at Rutgers to get a handle on who Valvano really was:*

When I got to school and into my dormitory, I saw this kind of crazy guy running around and laughing and yelling a lot all the time, and was also told that there was another basketball player who lived on the far side of the same floor. I remember thinking how this crazy guy's roommate was an intelligent, academic kind of guy who had his work cut out for him being the guy's roommate, and all the time I'm wondering when I'm going to meet this other basketball player on the same floor as me. It was like two or three days later that I learned that this wild and crazy guy was indeed the basketball player, and that all along his name was Jim Valvano.

Jim would drive you crazy, but you laughed. What I used to say was that living with Jimmy was like living with Henny Youngman. He was always *ba-da-bum, ba-da-boom* with another joke. That was my first impression of him. I was rooming with a guard that had been recruited out of New York, and he and I were the starters on the freshman team. So Jim guarded me every day in practice, and he was just a tenacious guy. To this day I say he's the toughest guy who ever guarded me, and we used to go at it pretty good. Then this other fellow got into academic trouble, so in the middle of our freshman season Jimmy and I started playing together in the backcourt. At that time, freshmen couldn't play varsity, so we spent the rest of our freshman year starting for the freshmen team and then spent all of the next three years as starters for the varsity team.

I think Jim would describe our playing together as him passing the ball and me shooting it. But Jim was a great defender and a very good ball handler. When you play with someone for that long, you get to know each other's game pretty well. When I drove to the basket, I always had a feel for where Jim was, and vice versa. It was a tremendous asset to play together for all three years in college. In our senior year I averaged like twenty-six or twenty-eight points a game and Jim averaged about fifteen or sixteen. When you look at college backcourts today you don't see many tandems averaging over forty points a game like we did. Also, that was without the three-point shot. More importantly, we knew what we could expect from the other person under pressure. A basketball game is just reacting, and if there's a split second of hesitation in trying to discern or understand what someone else if going to do, that's enough to cause a turnover.

∽∽∽

As serious and tenacious as he was when the ball was in play, Valvano also was a vocal leader who could inspire his team-mates as much with a wisecrack as he could with a crisp pass.
Lloyd:

Jimmy was always being funny. One of our teammates, Bob Greacen, used to joke, when someone asked him about what it was like having a guy like Jimmy on the bus, that "He needs a bigger bus." Jimmy did not change one iota from the time I knew him as an eighteen-year-old until the time he passed away. He was absolutely hysterical.

I remember one time I had two free throws when we were down by one point with just a few seconds to go. I made the first free throw but missed the second, and the game went into overtime. So in overtime, again, I get fouled with one second to go and we're down by one. Just before the ref gives me the ball to shoot my first free throw, I'm thinking, *Don't blow this one, Lloyd.* That's when Jimmy comes up to me, pats me on the butt, and says something to me. After the game, a reporter asked me what Jimmy had said to me at the free-throw line, if it had something to do with what we were going to do or whatever. And I said, "No, what he said to me, and this is the God's honest truth, was 'Lloyd, you got us into this mess; now get us out of it.'" It was Jimmy trying to relax me, and it worked. I made both shots and we won the game.

He was definitely the leader of our team. We were a young team. Jim really kept the younger players together and kept them encouraged. I was an All-American and going through all that kind of pressure of, like, *If I don't score twenty-five points, we're not going to win this game.* So Jim was the one who really kept everybody together.

⇜⇝

Bill Foster, *Valvano's coach at Rutgers, talks about Valvano the player:*

He just kept getting better and better as a player, and he and Bob Lloyd just got along so well. They had a wonderful relationship. Their relationship could have been made into a movie. When they were out there as players, people would want to know who the guy was with Bobby Lloyd, and as things turned around later on people would want to know who that guy was with Jim Valvano.

The thing was as Jimmy got better and better, he became a really fine player and ended up first-team all-NIT. When we went to the NIT for the first team, back when it was still a prestigious tournament, it was a great thing for Rutgers because I don't think we had been there, oh, maybe in forever. We opened with Utah State and then it was the New Mexico team that had Mel Daniels. The third game was a semifinal and we led Southern Illinois with Walt Frazier at halftime, but we lost. Then we played a high-scoring consolation game with Marshall and beat them, so we came in third. Bobby and Jimmy were both first-team all-NIT, and there were some really terrific players in the tournament that year, so that was really a feather in their cap.

The whole team got along well. It was a team, basically, of really good students, plus we sort of came from nowhere. Our first year there we had won something like five games more than the previous year's team and then we went 14–14, and I remember that that was the most wins Rutgers had had in nineteen years. Then along came Jimmy and Bobby, and we had some other good players such as Bob Greacen, who eventually played for the Milwaukee Bucks for a couple of years—he even got an NBA Championship ring. We were a nonscholarship school then, similar to the Ivy League, so it was a big deal.

Jimmy wasn't really highly recruited, but he just had a way about him in that he worked really hard, practiced well, and kept getting better. As much as he was lighthearted, he took basketball seriously and it really helped him and our team because he loosened everyone up. I probably got everyone nervous as hell, and Jimmy would take care of that.

I can remember one time coming back to school after we had won our first game in the NIT. We're getting off the bus and the cheerleaders and the students were out there to greet us, and the cheerleaders were kissing the ballplayers as they came off the steps of the bus. After Jimmy got off and got kissed, he ran back around to the back of the bus, somehow crawled back in, and came through the bus and back down the steps so that he could get another kiss from the cheerleaders. Even if he had any problems going on in his life, it was covered up by his lightheartedness.

⌒⌒⌒

Back in the sixties, the National Invitation Tournament was almost as prestigious as its NCAA counterpart with fewer teams in those days playing in each tournament. Rutgers, with Lloyd and Valvano leading the way, went to the NIT in 1967 and made it to the last two rounds played at Madison Square Garden. **Bob Lloyd** *offers this perspective:*

We played the NIT in the days when it was a significant tournament. The NCAA now has sixty-five teams in its tournament, and in those days I think it was less than half of that. You had teams that would have been ranked in the top thirty playing in the NITs, and it was even such that one year Al McGuire pulled his Marquette team out of the

NCAAs because he figured why should he be sending his team halfway across the country when he could keep his team close to home and take them to New York for the NIT. We had a great run before losing to Southern Illinois with Walt Frazier. Bill Foster was a great coach for us. Everyone knew what we were supposed to do and what our roles were; it was a good, solid-coached team that played multiple defenses.

☞

*It didn't take a genius to figure out that Valvano's basketball future beyond Rutgers was going to involve coaching, and **Lloyd** saw in his good friend a bright future patrolling the sideline:*

His father had been a coach and that's all he wanted to do. Jim and I used to talk about it a lot. One thing was that my older brother, Dick, had been an assistant for Bill Foster at Bloomsburg College in Pennsylvania and was then an assistant under Foster at Rutgers while we were there, so Dick shed some light on the coaching profession for Jim as well.

I can remember one time while we were there that one of our players, Bob Greacen, shaved his head for no apparent reason other than he felt like it. I said to Jim after practice, "I know I'm not going to have my livelihood depend on kids like 'Greek,'" even though I love Greek and he turned out to be a great coach and father. But Jimmy always wanted to be a coach, I think because of Rocco [Valvano's father].

But there were times that Jimmy didn't always get along with Bill [Foster]. At the end of our sophomore year, during which Jim had averaged something like twelve points a game, he went to Bill's basketball camp in the Poconos. One day Bill calls Jim into his office to talk to him. Later,

9

Jim comes back out on the court where I'm shooting the ball 'round and he's pretty livid. I asked him what happened, and he says, "Coach told me I get by on my natural athletic ability, that I can't touch the ball with my left hand, and that I could be a better shooter. I mean, here I am coming off a pretty good year and now he tells me that I'm not that good." And I said, "Well, Jimmy, he wants you to improve." Jimmy was still livid, and so what did he do? He spent the rest of the off-season practicing his shot and dribbling with his left hand, and he became a much, much better college basketball player. And then he became an assistant under Bill when he could have gone on to a lot of other places. He really respected and loved Bill.

After Jimmy first got into coaching, I would always tell people that he's going to be remembered like John Wooden. He's going to be remembered because he's a great coach and an intelligent coach. And if you remember, Jim was a master at using fouls at the end of the game to make the best use of his team because he didn't have the most talented team, even when his team won the national title in 1983. We were talking early in the tournament and he just kept saying, "If we can just keep it close, if we can just keep it close," and then when he gets ready to play in the Final Four, he says, "I don't know if I can make that work with these guys." But he did.

As soon as that last shot against Houston went through the basket, my phone rings and it's my brother Dick saying, "You know, I used to be known as the brother of the All-American guard, but now I'm going to be known as the brother of that other guard." It was very, very exciting.

⟨∞⟩

Lloyd and Valvano not only served time together as basketball teammates at Rutgers, they also served five and a half years together in the Delaware National Guard. **Lloyd:**
We saw each other most weekends, and we were even called out during the Martin Luther King riots, although I won't go into the stories about what our patrols were like.

∽∾∽

Tom Penders *has spent more than thirty years of his life as a basketball coach, most prominently in the college ranks at Columbia, Fordham, Rhode Island, Texas, and George Washington, following a path that early in his career often had him crossing paths with Valvano. They played against each other in college as opposing guards, Penders at Connecticut and Valvano at Rutgers, and they were even finalists once for the same job—at Columbia—which picked Penders over Valvano. Penders talks about his days of playing against Rutgers and Valvano:*

I played two years of varsity basketball against Jim, my junior year and my senior year, and we played the same position so we played head-to-head. It's not that we always guarded each other, but he brought the ball up and ran his team. He had Bob Lloyd in the backcourt with him who, my senior year, was one and two in the nation in scoring with a teammate of mine named Wes Bialosuknia. Wes and Bob were neck-and-neck all year long.

The last game of the season was in our place. Jimmy was joking the entire game and kept talking about the fact that with him having to guard Wes and me having to guard Bob, we were both in for a long night. And I loved him. He made me laugh when I played against him. We had some really

11

good games against each other. In his sophomore year, which was my junior year, we beat them at home and that cost them an NIT bid. And then the following year we played them and beat them at our place in our last game. We were a real powerful team, but that Rutgers team went pretty far in the NIT, which was a big tournament in those days.

Jimmy was a good player, but, man, he loved to talk. He loved to joke—he would talk the whole game long. I wouldn't call it trash. It was just Jimmy. He'd talk to the referees. He'd talk to anybody, but he did it in such a way that after the game was over you would seek him out to shake his hand. He was that kind of kid. Most of his humor was self-effacing. At the foul line he would say something and then start talking to himself. He was like a comic when he was playing. But he was good and he was very competitive and it was just Jimmy.

⌘

After playing four years at Rutgers, Valvano stuck around for two years as an assistant coach. Having Valvano as an assistant coach was even a no-brainer back when V was twenty-two and fresh out of college, as **Bill Foster** *recalls:*

Jimmy came from a great family in which everyone had a great deal of respect for one another, and that rubbed off on the team. You know, Nick [Valvano, Jimmy's older brother] was at Rider and then Bobby [Jimmy's younger brother] came along later and played. Bobby also went into coaching eventually. They had been sons of a coach, and Jimmy wanted to coach, so it was just natural for us to want to hire him at Rutgers as an assistant coach after he graduated. I don't remember if I approached him or if he came after the job—it was probably just sort of a combination of those two things.

It worked out well for us.

You could tell even then that he really handled players well as a coach; he related well to them. Then all of a sudden we get a call from Johns Hopkins for him to be a coach there, and from there to be an assistant at Connecticut. Johns Hopkins had to be a tough place for him because he was only twenty-four years old and had all these mature guys playing for him who were going to become doctors and such. But you could see him breaking out personality-wise, just gaining confidence with each passing year.

He would come back to be at the camps I had in the Poconos with Harry Litwack, so we would stay in touch that way. Jim would come back and eventually we got him to lecture, and he could hold an audience really well. Jim could get along with anybody, and he had a gift about him in exuding enthusiasm and confidence with his personality. It was really nice to see him go and progress as a coach. I kind of hated to see him at UConn because we played UConn, and while we had changed our defenses, we still used the same numbering system. Jimmy knew them as well as anybody did.

⁂

*After college **Tom Penders** gave professional baseball a shot and didn't see Valvano for a year or two. Penders then became a high school coach in the off-season, which brought him back into Valvano's world:*

By then, he was an assistant coach at UConn, so now he's at my alma mater and recruiting some of my high school players. And that was a real trip. Jimmy was also the freshman coach at UConn and he'd play my high school team, which was Bridgeport Central High School and ranked number one in

13

the state. So I saw a lot of him.

When we went up there (Storrs, Connecticut) to play, Jimmy was our host, and I could see why he was such a clear communicator because he was just the same way he had been as a player. He was a funny guy who could remember names. He remembered stories and situations, and in later years it was like a ritual at the Final Four for me to get together with Jim and Dick Stewart and Bill Foster. We would all get together, and Jimmy'd talk about playing against UConn in that last game at UConn. Jimmy would go into this whole thing of imitating Foster, who had been his coach at Rutgers, telling him how to guard Penders and what to do if he goes left or if he goes right, and what to do should he pull up for a shot, and on and on. By the time he was done, Bill had tears in his eyes he was laughing so hard.

∽∞∽

*The opening for the Columbia job in 1974 came down to Penders and Valvano, and **Penders** recalls what he believes was the decisive factor in his getting the job instead of V:*

Columbia had a really big committee that was interviewing coaching candidates. I mean, it was a huge committee that included the athletic director, deans at the school, students, and so forth. There were at least thirty people in this room. Someone on the committee later told me that Jimmy was so funny during his interview that they were concerned he wasn't serious enough to coach in a major league school. I, on the other hand, had been somewhat intimidated by the whole surroundings to the point where I was real serious about everything I said. I was talking about graduation rates, how tough coaching is, and that kind of thing, and all of a sudden I got the job.

Jimmy and I joked about it afterward, and he always used to say that if it hadn't been for Penders, there never would have been a Final Four in his life because he never would have made it out of Columbia. A year later he took the Iona job. Iona was perfect for him, and he was perfect for them—it was a great match. Jimmy came in there, and one of the first calls he made was to me to schedule us. Ivy League basketball was considered pretty darn good at the time, and so we started a series between Columbia and Iona, who as far as we knew had never played each other.

ᑲᘏᘏᕉ

Nick Valvano *says his younger brother Jimmy wanted to be a coach in part because their father, Rocco, had been one. Nick elaborates a bit on what it was like growing up Valvano:*

To some degree all of our family members grew up involved in teaching. Our dad was a teacher and I taught for ten years, and, of course, teaching is very much a part of being any kind of coach. Any job in which you manage people you have to be a teacher. That coupled with the ability to always remember where you came from makes it easier for you to relate to other people because you know what they're going through.

When he got sick, he was only in his mid-forties, and he was just starting to realize he could do all these other things. But I don't think coaching was ever out of his mind, even near the end, because he didn't like the way he had left North Carolina State and perhaps there was a sense there that he hadn't fulfilled his mission in coaching. There was always that part gnawing at him a bit. It's like anything else in this country: When you're well known and get accused of some-

15

thing, it's always on page one; but when the truth comes out exonerating you, it's buried on page twenty-five.

Our family is so close that there isn't a person in our family who didn't get affected by what Jim went through in his last year at N.C. State. It's a shame because it was a vocal minority that raised the issue. Just recently I read back through a *Sports Illustrated* article that talked about how minor the infractions they found were, and yet how it had affected not only Jim but also these school administrators. It's unfortunate. But I would remind Jimmy how lucky he was in all this, because he was so multitalented in being able to do all these things and would always have something to fall back on even if he never got back into coaching.

❦

*After putting in two years at Rutgers as an assistant, Valvano went to Johns Hopkins, and in his first job as a head coach led his team to a 10–9 record. But Johns Hopkins was just a quick stopover, as Valvano had a ladder to climb. He moved up to Connecticut to spend two years as an assistant under Dee Rowe before getting his second head-coaching job at Bucknell. **Paul Biko** had been a promising basketball player coming out of high school, a highly recruited star whose playing career was derailed when an auto accident resulted in a severely injured arm. So instead of going to a topnotch Division I program, he went to Bucknell, where a couple of years later his world collided with Jim Valvano. By then, Biko had quit playing basketball because of his bad arm, but Valvano convinced him to play one more year, talking Biko into it over beers at a frat party:*

Being with him was like magic. That's the kind of leadership he had. Some people hold the position of leader, but really aren't a leader. He truly was a leader. When he came to Bucknell, I was a broken-down basketball player and didn't want to play ball anymore. But once I got back into basketball with him, I couldn't wait to get to practice. He taught me the values inherent in the game and how they pass on into the rest of your life. He worked your butt off. He'd kill you. Accept the responsibility and don't give any excuses, was one of his credos. You knew what he would say, and he would give you courage.

I had the best year of my life when I came back out for basketball. I set a scoring record at Bucknell that season. He'd look at me and say, "Look, I know if you push yourself, it might hurt. But you're going to be a new player." And that's how he got me to come back out for the team. That season turned out to be the best season Bucknell had ever had—we ended up being one win away from being in the Big Dance [the NCAAs]. He took that program over the top, and it got to the point where you couldn't get your hands on a ticket to get into a game. Sure, it wasn't a gigantic gym, but to see it filled up and rockin' meant something special to us.

He brought out the best in you. Talk about the master motivator. I remember one stretch of games at Bucknell when we had lost several games in a row. Finally he said to us, "I'll tell you what, if you guys win nine games in a row, I'll suit up with you for the next game—this will set a school record and you'll be remembered—and I'll warm up the last game of the season with you." We did it and the gym was packed for that last game. He dressed up in a uniform, warmed up with us, and we went on to win that game, too.

He just had a knack for firing us up. Another time we were playing one of the big schools—it might have been Syracuse—and we were down twenty-seven points at the half—and he came into the locker room and, seeing us down, he said, "Ah, *now* I understand you guys. You think this is a football game and that you're down four touchdowns. Hmmm. That shouldn't be too hard to overcome." And with that he had us ready to play the second half.

There was still another time when we were playing some-one like Rutgers, I think. It came down to the last few seconds and I got fouled, and am now shooting a one-and-one. So the other team had three time-outs and they called all three to try and ice me. And there's Jimmy in the huddle saying to me, "You're going to make them, right? Because if you don't make them you're going to make us look like fools. This time when you go out there, right before the ref hands you the ball, I want you to turn around and look at me, because then I'm going to call a time-out." So he called a time-out on me, too, just to have some fun, and it relaxed me. That's the kind of guy he was. He would teach you that if at the end of the game we're close, we were going to win. Don't worry about it.

⌒⌒⌒

*Jim and **Pam Valvano** spent three years in Lewisburg, Pennsylvania, while he coached at Bucknell, and Pam remembers it as a picture-perfect setting and the epitome of what a college town should be:*

The campus is beautiful, and it really is a small-town atmo-sphere. It was hard when I moved there, but by the end of the three years we had made some really, really nice friends. I had more friends in the neighborhood that weren't involved with the college. A lot of times in the coaching business you go somewhere and most of your friends there end up being from the college or the university that you're at, although up there at Bucknell we made some friends who had nothing to do with the basketball program.

Being the wife of a basketball coach was tough. He missed a lot with the kids. He had a lot of times where he was gone and on the road. It's hard for every wife of a coach, whatever sport it might be. And the bigger the level, the higher the stakes, the tougher it is.

No matter where we were, Jim would always dream big, and his aspirations were always about winning big and winning the NCAA Championship, and he knew that he had to be at a certain level of school in order to be in position to do that. I tell people all the time that he always kept these little index cards, and he would always be writing on them what his goals and dreams were. He was very goal-oriented and knew what he wanted to do in his lifetime. Remember, he was an English major, and he never wanted people to think of him as a dumb jock. He could talk to you about politics; he could talk to you about books; he could talk to you about investments. He knew a lot about many things and that was what was so great about him—that he was not just a one-dimensional person.

He would always write on the index cards, and when I took his clothes to the dry cleaners, I would have to take his cards out so they wouldn't get ruined. The last index card I ever found said, "To find a cure for cancer." I still have that one.

⌒〜〜〜⌒

Tommy Thompson has been a coach at Bucknell for more than thirty years and as of 2001 was working as the school's golf coach. He was a basketball assistant for a number of years before Valvano arrived and stayed on as an assistant under Valvano. Thompson talks about his memories of Valvano and the Bucknell basketball program:

He put some excitement and energy into the program, even though he had a losing record for the three years combined he was here. But he got us over the hump.

I got to know him so-so. You could tell that this was just a short stop for him. He was a go-getter and the type of guy you knew was on his way to the big time. He needed more than what we had to offer, although we went on to have nineteen really good years under Charlie Woollum that included a couple of appearances in the NCAA Tournament.

Jim had a little trouble the first couple of years because, with the academic standards and the need-based scholarships, it was tough to go out and recruit that blue-chip kid. So we had to go with some kids who were good student-athletes but maybe weren't in the blue-chip category. He didn't have an opportunity to bring in his own assistant coaches because at that time a lot of us had to coach more than one sport. I was head baseball coach and freshman basketball coach then, too.

I was a little bit older than he was and he leaned on me a lot because he was sort of a young coach. I was more of a steadying influence on him, the elder statesman, because he was a very excitable guy. If he got down on things a little, I was the guy to help pick him up.

He was a very charismatic guy and very good with motivation. He even suited up with the guys for one of the games and went out before the game and did lay-ups with them. He was also a very funny guy; he had people in stitches. He was the street-tough, good-talking kid who had been around the city. That was his drive: to get to the top. Lewisburg is a laid-back community and Jim was more from the New York City stuff, and he needed to get back there. And the thing that helped him at Iona was that he was their athletic director, too, and there was no football to deal with. Basketball was pretty much the sport, and when he got Jeff Ruland that pushed him over the top.

I still remember watching that national-championship game when he was at N.C. State. It was almost like it was fate for him to win that year, because he probably should have been out in the first round of the ACC Tournament.

⌒✎✎✎⌒

Fred Davis, one of a number of Washington, D.C.–area high schoolers who would try to play college ball for Valvano, played basketball at Bucknell before Valvano's arrival and tried unsuccessfully to hang on after Valvano took over the program. Davis talks about Bucknell, which is located in Lewisburg in central Pennsylvania:

A couple of Baltimore Colts players had graduated from there, including the great tight end Tom Mitchell, so I knew about Bucknell, and the athletics appealed to me. It's a beautiful school. I walked on to the team as a freshman, and scholarships, then as now, were all given on a financial-need basis. My parents sacrificed to send me. But I wanted to play and I made the freshman team and played some. It just so happens that one of the other players on the team was a young man by the name of Algin Baylor Garrett—Elgin Baylor's nephew. And on the varsity team that year was John Ramsay, son of Dr. Jack Ramsay, the NBA coach.

Bucknell is located right on the Susquehanna River, an hour's drive north of Harrisburg, the state capital. Back then the student body numbered around twenty-eight hundred, and today it's about thirty-three or thirty-four hundred. It's one of the best academic institutions in the country and is now a member of the Patriot League. The campus is adjacent

21

to the downtown; that is, you can walk from the gym to the main street in ten minutes. The surrounding community is made up of about seven or eight thousand people, and it's a very historic town, so you're talking about Mayberry. It's a real quaint, cute little town. Within ten miles of Lewisburg there are some Amish communities. You'd see the little buggies on the side of the road.

❦

Davis talks about how Valvano's arrival at Bucknell renewed hope in the basketball program, although it didn't do much for Davis's future in the sport:

I made the varsity team as a walk-on my sophomore year, and this was when we had Don Smith as our coach. I was six-foot-two and tried to play guard, but I really wasn't quick enough, and yet I really wasn't big or strong enough to play forward. Offensively, however, I was a really good shooter, although you wouldn't want me out there trying to stop the best player on the other team, if you get my drift. So after my sophomore year along comes Coach Valvano as our new head coach, and I figured, *Well, here's a new coach and maybe he can make good use of me, even with my limited abilities.* I figured I would try out again and give Bucknell basketball one more shot. But none of us really knew anything about him and therefore didn't know what to expect.

I had a tryout, it was a two-day tryout, and there were about twenty guys going out for twelve or thirteen spots. Basically, tryouts consisted of scrimmages in the gym, open to the public, open to the students. Anybody could come in and watch, and Valvano just sat there off to the side watching us. He mixed and matched guys to get different looks at all of us. When it was over, instead of putting up a list of who made the team, he called each one of us into his office to tell us one-on-one whether or not we had made the team and why. That was a pretty classy thing to do, when he could have taken the easy way out.

I had played really well during the tryout. I had taken the ball away from a couple of guards and had hit a bunch of shots. I was in a groove. And it was fun, too. It was exciting. Jimmy V called me in and he says, "Fred, I just want to tell you that I really like you and I like your attitude. I know you've been with this program for a couple of years and you're a walk-on." He was very gracious and he complimented me on giving to the program while knowing that I wasn't getting any money from the school, blah, blah, blah. Then he gets to the point: "You know, it's my first year and I have a certain philosophy and you're a great kid and I'd love to keep you on the team, but I just don't have enough jerseys. If this was another year and it wasn't my first year, perhaps I'd keep you around. You know you don't really have the quickness to play, and I just can't afford the luxury of a shooter." And I accepted that. I wasn't expecting to be a starter, but I thought I could be an asset as an outside shooter, perhaps coming into the game as a zone buster. In any event, I didn't make the team.

After that, because it was a small campus, I'd see Jimmy around all the time. His first team was pretty average, but one thing about them was that they didn't shoot the ball well from the field. It was pretty much the same thing the next year, and in the back of my mind I'm thinking that he could have used me. Anyway, one night I was walking through the student center on the way back to my fraternity house, and Coach V comes out of the snack bar there and I run into him. He stops and says, "Hi, Fred. How are you?"

I go, "Hi, Coach, how are you doing?" And he said, "You know, we could have used your jump shot this year," meaning my senior year, and I said, not gruffly or in a mean way, "Coach, you could have used my jump shot last year." And he nodded and said, "You got me."

I like to kind of brag about that now. It was 1973 when he cut me from the team, and then it was 1983 when he won that national title at N.C. State. I tell people how Coach V was the guy who cut me, but obviously he learned a lot in ten years.

At Bucknell, he had been a young coach trying to get traction for a career at a school that doesn't emphasize athletics. And so he did fine, and he got along fine there. But, you know, that wasn't going to be his calling. I would still go to a lot of practices even when I wasn't on the team anymore, and he was really energetic. He'd have a whistle in his mouth and would run the length of the court the whole time, showing the kind of shape he was in. He would yell encouragement and was very positive, all the time.

As active as he was on the sideline during games as well as practices, he was always under control. In those days, coaching wasn't quite the micro-managed thing it is today; you just took the kids out there and let them play. Today, guys are signaling plays every time up the court. It has become a much more tightly scripted game.

⟨✦⟩

Ken Lambert, Valvano's first student manager at Bucknell, had actually seen Valvano play ball at Rutgers although he didn't know who Valvano was at the time, only that he had a teammate named Bob Lloyd, who was the star of the Rutgers team.

Lambert offers his recollections of Valvano and how he arrived at Bucknell with the intent of turning around a lackluster program:

I had been the team manager for three years before Valvano arrived at Bucknell as coach. His predecessor was Don Smith, who was kind of at the tail end of his career and had been through some losing seasons, so the morale of the team at that time was not good. The players felt that they had been better than the scores indicated, and if they just had a better coach, things would improve.

Remember, this was at a school where the basketball team was made up essentially of walk-ons and merit scholars—those who got scholarships based on need. Our big games were against teams like Lehigh, Colgate, and Lafayette, and we even played Penn State for a while. Don Smith was an incredibly nice man, but our basketball team was almost like a joke. He just didn't have it in him at that point to build the team up. He couldn't inspire enthusiasm or confidence, and I think [the administration] wanted somebody who was kind of cool to coach. Valvano provided that answer almost immediately.

That's what I noticed when he came in: here was a guy who wore interesting clothes, who listened to the music kids were listening to, and he'd recently been a player himself. And so he was tuned in. He had a pretty wife, little kids, and we would go over to his house for pizza a couple of times. We never did that with the other coach. The team trips on the bus were more fun, and the meals were more fun when we went to away games—he was just a lot more fun to be around. So it was an interesting contrast; I guess that's how I would put it.

*As much as **Lambert** was intrigued by what Valvano brought to Bucknell, he had mixed feelings about his year there working under Coach V:*

I could sense that this was a small town, not the big lime-light that he craved, and he certainly got that later on. I was glad he got that championship at N.C. State, and I rooted for them all the way, like, "There's Valvano: I managed for him!" I was thrilled. That was the most exciting champion-ship run I've ever seen, and I've watched them every year. I'm glad it was him, I really am.

The Bucknell thing, though, I'd almost rather forget. Ironically, I had better experiences there with the earlier coach [Don Smith], who had been much nicer to me. Whenever I ran into Valvano as an alumnus, it was kind of awkward because I wasn't too interested in talking to him. I stayed in Lewisburg for two years after I graduated because my girlfriend was still going to school there. I'd go down to some of the practices and the games, or I'd see him around campus every once in a while. He'd say, "Hi, Kenny, how ya doing?" and I'd say, "Fine." But there never was this warmth other people talk about. I wish I had experienced it. But I didn't get to.

There was a mixed bag there. He goosed up that place to a certain extent and made it more fun. But on the other hand, he used it, too. But that's how people get ahead. There were some players there who went away unhappy. Our cen-ter, our leading player, was Harvey Carter who was about six-foot-six and he played three really good years, the first two under Smith, and we thought Valvano would really turn him loose. But he hurt his knee during the season and played a lot on an injured knee. Harvey had surgery after the season, and he was pretty upset with Valvano and the whole basketball situation. He felt he had played too much on a bad knee to help the team get as many wins as possible, and this was a guy who was never going to play in the pros and was going to school on a scholarship based on need.

All things considered, the program took off under Valvano, and then Charlie Woollum took it over for many years and built on it and kept it going.

∾

Paul Biko, who first got to know Valvano when they were at Bucknell in the mid-seventies, said that the outgoing Valvano the public was introduced to after his N.C. State team won the 1983 national title was no different than the effervescent Valvano he had played for years earlier. Valvano didn't change in the limelight; it's just that more people after 1983 were seeing him in that light for the first time:

Before he was well-known to the American public, Jim had always been the same way—an outgoing and personable guy drawing a lot of attention, yet being loyal and close to his players. One of the things that used to bother me after the national title was that people who didn't know any better thought he was coming on like this because of all the attention he was now getting, when in fact he had *always* been like that, even when there wasn't a single camera or microphone in front of him. What people saw as the media-fed, overnight star was no different from what he had been a decade earlier.

He wanted to get into broadcasting, that was his dream. Put him in front of people and he was magic. Yet his family was vitally important to him. When he was in line for the UCLA job in the late eighties, he was really wrestling with it, and we talked about it over the phone. He took Pam and the girls out there on a visit, and they didn't really like it out there. He called me and said, "You know it's a great opportunity, but I can't hurt my family."

I think he got taken advantage of by some people in the business world because he had this heart that was bigger than gold. He was a giver, and some people took advantage of it.

⌒∞∞⌒

As a basketball player at Bucknell, Biko had a second family, and it was the Jim Valvano family. When you played for Valvano, he would have you over to his house to meet Pam and the girls, and he wasn't just going through the motions of being an accommodating guy. Valvano wanted you at his house, and his players enjoyed being there, as **Biko** *recalls:*

It was an unbelievable, beautiful family. We would go over there for dinner, just so he could get to know you. Once you were on the team, you were part of his family. You didn't often find it in that day and age that you could be close to someone in such a situation, but Jimmy wasn't your typical guy. He really cared about people and especially about his players and his family.

In this setting, he would tell us things like: "It's easy to have faith and a positive attitude when you are on top, but what you've gotta have is faith and a positive attitude when you're not on top. That's how you become a winner."

⌒∞∞⌒

*After **Biko** left Bucknell and Valvano moved on to Iona and then N.C. State, Biko followed him some, working with Valvano on a few business ventures:*

I was going to be an engineer, but he talked me into being a basketball coach. I took a high school job, and he was nice enough to come up and speak at our awards banquet. I didn't have to pay him anything. He would drive up, give a great speech, and just help you out because he loved doing it so much.

Then I got into business, and he said, "Good. You stay in business and I'll stay in coaching, and we'll run some businesses together that way." And that's what we did. I started off in the insurance business, and we created a national advisory board. We hired coaches and teachers to work for us, and we'd put together a clinic to be held at a place that he picked out for us, and he would run the clinic. The magnetism he had—unbelievable.

As a coach, the power of his passion was second to none. That's why he was able to get so much out of his team late in a game. He had that dream of being a national-championship coach, and he shared that with me: "This is the amount of work I'm going to have to put into it, and this is what it's going to cost me." He said, "If you do the same thing: put in a plan and work as hard as you can in following it, you will be able to accomplish something, too."

In a game, he would know every weakness of the other team. I didn't know it at the time, but he must have spent an awful lot of time studying the videos. In terms of passion and knowledge of the game, he ranked right there with anybody. He could look at an opponent, say, Temple, which had a great matchup zone defense, and he would make the effort to know that matchup zone as well as anyone could. That separated him from most guys. He'd take the time to set up the plan and make sure that we could work it to perfection. That confidence he had in himself about knowing what to do was something he was able to pass on to players. I remember one time we were down nine points with forty-seven seconds left in the game, and he told us, "All right, we've got 'em right where we want them." And he's laughing. He's sincere.

He had this saying about working to get ahead, that even if you enter a revolving door behind somebody, he'd find a way to come out of it ahead of him.

*When Valvano left Bucknell to take the Iona job in 1975, he inherited a program in desperate need of a fix, as **Rich Petriccione**, Iona's vice-president for advancement–external affairs and in those days a student manager under Valvano, recalls:*

When he got here, we had the worst record in America. We had been something like 6–19 or 6–20 the season before, which I think had been the worst record in Division I. And then five years later, when he left, we were 29–5 and ranked nineteenth in the final Associated Press poll of 1980. That was the season in which we beat the eventual national champion Louisville in the [Madison Square] Garden, when we were seventeen-point underdogs. We beat them by seventeen.

He took us to a place we'd never been before. When I was a senior in high school, Iona beat Saint John's for the first time in something like forever. He and Louie [Saint John's coach Lou Carnesecca] were real close, but it was like, you don't do that to the godfather. He got us to where people would now look at Iona as a solid, major program on the verge of breaking through. His minimum standard for a season was twenty wins and a post-season bid. The biggest thing that he did for us was that he got Jeff Ruland to come here. Jeff was a legitimate first-team, All American high school player—a McDonald's All American. He was being pursued by Kentucky, Indiana, Notre Dame . . . and Iona. Jimmy did all this on the whole concept of daring to dream, being a big fish in a small pond, and doing something that nobody would have thought possible.

◦⟩⟩⟩⟩◦

Six-foot-eleven center **Jeff Ruland** *was the first genuine blue-chip recruit Valvano ever landed, and it was with Ruland that Valvano turned little Iona College into something of a basketball power in the late seventies. Ruland could have gone to almost any school in the country, and Kentucky was hot on his heels, but Valvano was able to convince him to join him in living a dream at Iona, where Ruland now toils as head basketball coach:*

During my senior year in high school, we had just had a two-week layover during Christmas, and in our first game after break there were a bunch of college coaches in the stands who were there to watch me play. And I was terrible. I must have mishandled the ball four or five times while trying to shoot, and it was just not a good game for me at all. But after the game, all these coaches were coming up to me and telling me how great a game I had played, and then here comes Valvano up to me and he says, "Man, you sucked!" Right then I knew I liked this guy. He was the only coach who was being totally honest with me, and I appreciated that.

I lived on Long Island, only forty-five minutes from the Iona campus, and never actually made an official visit there.

But what I would do is drive over there about once a week to visit with Coach V. He was like a father to me, or an uncle or a big brother—however you want to put it. My own dad had died years earlier, and my stepfather was a real jerk. I didn't have a father figure in my life, and Jim was someone

Valvano in 1977 looking Saturday Night Fever*ish as he guides his Iona team in a game against the University of Detroit. (AP/Wide World Photos)*

who could fill that gap for me. He was only about thirty years old then, so there wasn't a huge age gap between us either.

I had no trouble deciding that Iona was where I wanted to go, even though the campus today is a much nicer place than it was twenty years ago. The only appeal it had then was that you could walk out the front gate and find six or seven bars within a few blocks of campus. I mean, this place supposedly had fifty-five acres to it, and I've always wondered where thirty or so of those acres were because I didn't see them. What he sold me on was his dream, and that's something he was always able to sell players on. It was a dream of winning the national championship and how a bunch of guys from Long Island—which is where he grew up—could come together at Iona and do great things. I was sold on this and saw this as more of a challenge for me than going to Kentucky. I guess you could say it was that crazy New Yorker mentality.

∽∾

*The apex of Valvano's coaching career prior to the 1983 national-title season at N.C. State was the 1979-80 season at Iona when he, Ruland, and guard Glenn Vickers led the Gaels to a 29-5 season and the school's first-ever foray into the national rankings. Iona finished the season 29-5 after losing in the second round of the NCAA Tournament to Georgetown. Following the season, Valvano took the North Carolina State job, and in the process alienated himself from Ruland, in part over a misunderstanding involving an alleged exchange of cash between an agent and Ruland. There was also some grief caused when news of Valvano's impending departure for N.C. State leaked before he had had a chance to tell his players. **Ruland:***

It was a bittersweet season. We had some good wins along the way, such as when we beat Kansas and then Louisville in the [Madison Square] Garden, but we should have been a Final Four team. There was a jealousy factor among some of the players, and we didn't achieve all that we were capable of.

The highlight was the game against Louisville: It fulfilled Coach V's dream of playing in the nine o'clock game at the Garden, playing in front of nineteen thousand people. Before the game, he said to me, "Can you picture it, Rules? Can you picture it?" Funny thing, though: Although we jumped into the top-twenty rankings at number eighteen or nineteen after we beat Louisville, we won two or three games the following week and dropped out of the rankings. Go figure. It's pretty sick when you think about it.

What happened between us after that season put a rift between us for a number of years, and I'm sorry that we never really smoothed everything over. He had questioned my loyalties back at Iona and I didn't handle it well, and I only wish I had it all to live over again. I was going to go down and see him to make amends with him, but I never got that chance.

ᑭᗰᗰᑎᕐ

Linda Bruno, commissioner of the Atlantic 10 Conference, was an administrative assistant for Valvano at Iona in the late seventies, beginning soon after she had graduated from there with a degree in English:

I taught eighth-grade English in the Bronx for a year and didn't like it, so I went back to Iona that summer and started work on my master's degree. I went out one night with some friends to a restaurant, and in walks J. B. Bruno, the Iona athletic trainer, and I started talking to him, saying, "I really don't know what I want to do other than finish my master's degree." And that's when he said, "You know, Jim Valvano, who happens to be the basketball coach, is looking for people to work in the department." And the deal was that if you went to school while you worked there, you could go to school for free.

I applied for a job there. Jim called me a few days later and said, "The only job I really have open is a secretarial position," and I said, "I really don't have any secretarial skills"—that I was an English major who typed her own papers and that's about it. And he said, "Oh, you're an English major!" And so we talked for about ten minutes about how we both were English majors and probably weren't going to use our degrees the way they were intended to be used.

I went in to meet him and he called me back a few days later and said, "I'd love to have you," and I said, "Just so you're clear, I really just want this job until I get my master's degree because I think I want to go back and teach." He said, "That's fine." And that's how I ended up working with him.

He was everything that was fun about athletics. The joke of the whole thing—and we used to joke about this later on—was that I didn't have any clerical skills. And he was very patient with me. After I got my masters, I started joking that he had to promote me so that he could get a real secretary and get something done in the department. So from there I actually went on to do some of the academic advising in the department and I sold tickets and did scheduling—all kinds of things. It just would never happen that way now. Never in a million years, because everyone is so specialized. He was one of those people who could make you happy about coming to work. He really did.

☙

Bruno offers this description of Iona College and what kind of setting Valvano spent five years soaking up while honing his coaching skills for the future jump to the "big time":

I'm on [Iona's] board of trustees right now, which I'm sure has Jim just turning over in his grave. It's really kind of interesting for me as I still keep in touch with the school. It's a wonderful place. It's a small school, a Catholic college. It's in a very nice area in Westchester County, which is upscale. It is south of New York City with all those benefits. You really don't have any of those problems that have become associated with the city.

At the time, when I went to school there, which is before Jim arrived, they'd play their basketball games at Iona Prep. When Jim became basketball coach my senior year, the new facility was built—a place with about four thousand seats. It's very small with a campus cozy enough to where everybody knows everybody else. Even now when I go back for meetings and such, I still run into some of the same people. It's a very warm place, it really is.

◁▩▷

Bruno says Iona's cozy atmosphere was a perfect backdrop for Valvano to be the Big Man on Campus:

He really was larger than life, particularly in that environment. He was very well-liked, though, even by the faculty. I could tell that from my work as an academic advisor, and that's a position in which you can really become at odds with the academic side of things and conflicts really do exist. But with his personality, Jim was always able to work through those issues, and that's because the faculty deep down knew he really did care about the kids.

He was always concerned about them on the court, but he also wanted them to get degrees. He told them it was very important that they went to class. And in fact he was the one that was so adamant about establishing some kind of academic advisement program within the athletic department when I was there.

I always thought that he could do whatever he wanted to. You know, he's very, very talented. You never worried about Jim.

I think I picked up a little bit of my sense of humor from him, and I also think that when things occasionally get rough, like going through a difficult issue at work, you can remember back to what he stood for and think, *Thank God, we're not dealing with life or death issues, you know, we're dealing with college athletics.*

To me, his legacy was that he made you feel good about what you were doing. Sometimes people don't. He always made you feel that way, like *Maybe we lost tonight, but we're going to win in two days.* After losses he would be the one in the department the next day picking people up.

I used to tease him because after he lost he would love to come into work and actually do some administrative work to get his mind off coaching. He said, "That's my part of the department that is most productive." And he actually sat and worked through some things. But the thing that's really amazing to me is that when you meet a guy like him, so fun-loving, funny, and outgoing, you assume he has a personality that is not detail oriented, and nothing could be further from the truth with Jim. He was so smart and nothing ever fell through the cracks. The more you worked with him the more you realized that.

Valvano's five years at Iona brought him closer to home than any of his other jobs, but that proximity to home, for a while, wasn't all that it was cracked up to be. **Pam Valvano:**

We were made to feel at home there—the Irish Christian brothers were really wonderful to us, and Brother John Driscoll [Iona's president] was so good to me that I can't tell you. But when we first moved there, we had to live about forty-five minutes away from the school, and the roads [from snow and ice, or just snarled traffic] were so horrible that if Jim couldn't get home at night, he would just sleep in his office. There were some times it was just too icy for him to try driving home, and a lot of times I couldn't come to the games because of the road conditions and my responsibilities as a mother with two young girls. So I felt very isolated from the school and the program, where before we had always lived very close to the campus. The taxes and housing costs were so high in New Rochelle around the school that we couldn't afford to live nearby. We had to go forty-five minutes out to be able to afford to buy a house.

We lived out there for a year. Brother Driscoll felt bad that we lived so far away and that I felt so isolated, so he made it possible for us to rent a home owned by the school in that area near Iona. Now it was a matter of Jim being close to work, and the girls and I could once again be a part of all of it.

Iona vice-president for advancement–external affairs **Rich Petriccione**, *a basketball student manager at Iona College while*

Valvano was a coach there, recalls how they quickly became good friends, even with an age difference of about ten years:

The first time I ever met him was my first day of college. I went up to the gym and I, literally, met him right in front of the building. I knew who he was because I had been to a couple of games the previous year, and I had seen his name and picture in the paper. I remember thinking he was kind of a strange-looking dude. You know, he had this incredible forehead and big nose, and back then he had a bad haircut. He looked like Herman Munster with the bangs, and then he had the big nose. Joe Namath has a big nose, too, V said, but the difference is that they call Namath "ruggedly handsome," which Jim really wasn't. And I remember introducing myself to him and telling him that I wanted to work with the team and I thought I could help him.

There was a kid at my high school who was a year behind me named Jimmy Black, who would go on to play at North Carolina and help them win the national championship. And so one of the first things I told Coach was that I could help him get Jimmy Black to come to Iona, although it didn't quite turn out that way. Oh, we got him signed to a letter of intent, but that was in the days when letters of intent weren't really binding, and he ended up going to North Carolina instead.

We hit it off right away. He made me an office manager and a student assistant to help him, and like most coaches he was very dependent on those type of people to take care of mundane things like getting kids to school and picking up dry cleaning. It quickly became clear that one of the things he loved was having an audience, and I was a very good audience for him because I couldn't get enough of him. I just absolutely loved hanging out with the guy.

My school day for the three years that I was there with him would literally be to get to school about eight in the morning. I would drive in from the Bronx and either just go find him or go to the office, or sometimes I would join him and take his kids to school or join him and [assistant coach] Pat Kennedy and we'd get the players to school. Other than the time I had to be in classes, I was with him just about all the time. And it was just an unbelievable experience for a young kid.

This was when he was not famous. He was very funny, gutsy, aggressive, egomaniacal, and entertaining. I'll never forget when he had to go scout Farleigh Dickinson in Jersey, and it was only a half-hour ride from Iona. And he wanted me to go with him. It was the first time we had ever been alone together for a good period of time. On the car ride over I was just floored by the way he would just open up. I mean, he didn't really know me that well. And that was the first time that he gave me the whole spiel about how "I'm going to win the national championship someday. I'm going to make a million dollars. And, I'm going to be on the *Johnny Carson Show*. And I think what I'd like to do after I win the championship is to do something like what this guy Bob Uecker did and get my own TV sitcom, because that's where the real money is." I just remember sitting in the front seat of the car—it was an old Ford—listening to all this and thinking just how incredible it was.

❧

Petriccione saw Valvano not only as a mentor, but as a sort of Renaissance man who loved to soak up knowledge:

Jim really loved to [learn]. He loved to exercise his brain, and he loved to read. He'd really get into poetry. On the team bus he would quote E. E. Cummings one minute and the next he would be doing the stupidest, silliest stuff. He'd do anything to get a laugh. He literally would do anything. He would do slapstick; he would do physical comedy; he would even pull the old finger and fart stuff—anything to make you laugh. He was crazy; he was a true character. He strived to be different. His career really paralleled [football coach] Lou Holtz's in many ways in that he dreamed things and then accomplished them.

Did you ever hear the [Ronald] Reagan story? Jim was so bold, and sometimes he couldn't help himself. So here he is at the White House after N.C. State won the national championship. They're all sitting there nervous, waiting on the president. Suddenly the Secret Service guys touch their earpieces and in walks Reagan. He sits down next to Jim, shakes his hand, and says, "Congratulations, Coach. And tell me, is it Val-VAY-no or Val-VAH-no." And without hesitation Jim says, "I don't know. Is it REE-gun or RAY-gun?" And then, I'm told, the president gave Jim one of those looks like, *What are you, a jerk?* Later Jim goes, "I just couldn't help it. How the hell would the guy who invited me to the White House not know how to say my name? What, did he live in the backhills?" But that's what he did. His brain worked differently.

↩↩↩

Valvano not only was a topnotch basketball coach, he also had been a good player, as **Petriccione** *found out at Iona:*

Jim prided himself on being an athlete. When I was a student working a summer basketball camp with him, every morning before that day's camp actually started for the kids, like from eight to nine, he and I would wave over any two kids in camp and challenge them to a game of five points or whatever, and then it became a matter of having to beat these kids. If I missed a shot or something, he would really scream at me. Winning was really important to him.

Off the court, his philosophy was to enjoy life and learn about different things, but for those forty minutes of a game, winning was the most important thing in the world. He would try and get everybody to really think, to really concentrate for those forty minutes on what we had to do and what would help us be successful. But the minute the game was over, he used to try and bring us back down by telling everybody how completely insignificant the game we had just played was. He would talk about some major event in the world or how much our parents loved us. He would take it from one end of the spectrum at the beginning of the game, when he needed full use of your mind, your body, your spirit, and your soul, to the other end of the spectrum. At the end saying, "Now that was fun, wasn't it?"

⧞

Jeff Ruland summarizes Valvano the coach and what made him tick:

He was a great motivator, but he certainly was no great Xs and Os guy, at least not then [in the late seventies]. I could learn more from my high school basketball coach than from him, but no coach I had ever known could motivate the way Coach V could. He and I really had a unique relationship. I'd walk up and he'd start diagramming plays on the board while telling me all that he could teach me about playing center, and I would just roll my eyes. But all things considered, he could really get your best performance out of you.

You should have seen him in practice. One time he would be out there with us, leading us on the three-on-two fast break drill. Then another time he might stop practice so we could go outside and have a snowball fight. And when he wasn't doing that, he might be at the local bar with us downing a few brews and talking all about how great we could be. I remember one time when we were on the bus coming back from a game, and he had the bus stop outside a club so that we could go inside and have some fun. He was that kind of guy, a good family man who loved Pam and his daughters, but who also cared enough about his players to spend time with them, and I guess you could say he had trouble growing up. I'm the same way to this day, and I have three daughters and a twenty-year marriage of my own, to boot.

༄༅

Rich Petriccione, *who also was Iona's athletic director for twelve years, saw Valvano as not only a great motivator, but also as a coach adept with the Xs and Os:*

I don't think he ever got enough credit for being a good coach, not only during the games, but at halftime he was great at making adjustments. He used to tell us that you can't just practice your offense and think that's going to be good enough. And he coached by the seat of his pants, sometimes throwing in triangles and changing the defense every time down the floor.

༄༅

As the wife of Jim Valvano, **Pam Valvano** *was frequently on the go as her coaching husband went from Rutgers to Johns*

Hopkins to Connecticut to Bucknell and on to Iona in the space of less than ten years. But it's a small world, as Pam found out at Iona during the 1979-80 season, when the Gaels went to the NCAA Tournament and ended up playing their early round games at Reynolds Coliseum in Raleigh, which less than a year later would be their new home:

I went with Jim on that trip and remember driving around Raleigh thinking, *Wow, this could be a neat place to live: I really like it down here.* Little did I know that I would be coming back and living there within a few months. It is so weird sometimes how things work out.

We moved here in 1980 and I had a five-week-old, an eight-year-old, and an eleven-year-old, but it was probably the easiest of all the moves for me because the people down here, even though we were northerners, were wonderful to us. I just met so many nice people, and it was a very, very easy transition for me even though I had a new baby and I didn't know anybody. And the ten years that he coached here [N.C. State] were for the most part wonderful times. Even after he left the university, we couldn't think of any other place we really wanted to move to, so we decided to stay here, in part because by now we had a lot of close friends here. We were really, really happy here.

༄

*As driven as he was, Valvano would always call a number of people close to him to get their thoughts when he was going after another coaching job, and one of those confidants was older brother **Nick Valvano**:*

Every job he was going to take, or was at least considering, he would call to talk. He'd talk, I'd listen, just to have someone who would be objective about what he was thinking about instead of just going to our dad and having him say to Jim, "Hey, whatever you want to do, I'm behind you 100 percent." So every step along the way, we always talked.

I think the most difficult one was when he was leaving Iona for N.C. State. For lots of reasons. It was New York, the school [Iona] had treated him very well, he had great success there, and he was very close to his players there. Leaving there was the hardest thing in the world, but the ACC is the ACC—the best basketball conference in the country. I think his inexperience showed in that because he didn't handle the discussion well, and it somehow leaked to the press in New York before he had had a chance to talk to his players. It got out of hand. That was the hardest one for him.

The other moves were a part of his getting to a point. He had to leave Rutgers because he didn't want to be an assistant anymore, so he goes to Johns Hopkins and becomes the youngest head coach in Division I. I knew he wasn't going to stay there long. He liked Connecticut as an assistant, but he needed to get back into head coaching, so he went to Bucknell. He stayed there three years, and then it was on to Iona.

While he was at Iona, he was tipped off that the Big East was about to be created and that Iona was probably not going to be a part of it. And if Iona was not going to be a part of the Big East, then he knew he wasn't going to be able to compete for the same players that he was now getting to go to Iona. One person involved in all this was trying to get Jimmy to go to Providence and told Jimmy that Saint John's would probably be the only New York City school to be in the Big East. At that point, I'm sure Jimmy's thinking, *What am I going to do?* Then this chance with N.C. State comes along. Career-wise, it was the right move, but the way he left Iona hurt him a lot. And when N.C. State came up here the next year to play Iona at Madison Square Garden in the ECAC Holiday Festival, the fans really let Jim have it. They booed him, and some people actually threw things at him as he walked to the court.

2

N.C. STATE AND THE CARDIAC PACK

Jim Valvano's window of great opportunity, in his case the college basketball big time, probably was not going to stay open for long. Iona was not in position to become a perennial top-twenty program capable of averaging more than twenty victories a season. So if Valvano was going to achieve his dream of winning a national championship, it would have to be with a program capable of gathering the talent and consistently competing in a league at a level in which national titles were achievable, not practically impossible. North Carolina State, which had won an NCAA title as recently as 1974 and belonged to the elite Atlantic Coast Conference [ACC], was that once-in-a-career chance for Valvano, and he jumped for it when the position was offered him.

The eighties were a decade that gave us a New Wave sound in music, Michael Douglas on cinematic Wall Street saying, "Greed is good," and the debate over Star Wars technology in an era in which the Cold War actually was winding down. In a sense, Jim Valvano was the perfect icon for the eighties, a one-man personification of what described the decade. His ten-year run at N.C. State began with the advent of the eighties and ended with the start of the nineties, and in between he became a rich man, as far as college basketball coaches go, with fattened shoe contracts and weekly radio/TV shows. He brought Vinnie Barbarino-like youthful exuberance and brash confidence into what was pretty much a Mr. Woodman-like staid, buttoned-down ACC built on old-school traditionalism. Valvano's N.C. State teams won a national title [1983], made it all the way to two other Elite Eights [1985 and 1986], averaged twenty-one victories a year, and gave a whole new meaning to how to steal victories in the final sixty seconds. Valvano's Wolfpacks never achieved a Carolina/Duke type of dominance, but his teams scraped, scrapped, and sometimes even laughed their way to the kind of successes that only a Valvano could inspire.

While he was at N.C. State, Valvano became bigger than life. He was a celebrity whose star power transcended basketball, and yet no major college basketball coach was as approachable and down to earth as he was. He could light up a room in which the door was always open. His talents as an entertainer went beyond the basketball court, yet basketball coaching was what surged through his veins. Even after he left N.C. State under a dark cloud of an NCAA investigation that packed more drama than evidence, Valvano, like his dad before him, remained a basketball coach at heart. Even in a second career as a quickly successful and energized TV basketball commentator, Valvano never was far removed from coaching rumors, such as one that had him going to Wichita State.

Valvano not only craved the excitement of college basketball, he was one of its primary sources. For *most* of his tenure at N.C. State, he was Mr. Excitement. Much of the last two years of Valvano's reign at N.C. State was a miserable time for him. First, a book called *Personal Fouls* came out accusing Valvano and N.C. State of a variety of indiscretions, and the resultant fallout included an NCAA investigation of Valvano's basketball program. The investigation found, simply, that players had sold complimentary game tickets and basketball shoes for cash. For this relatively minor infraction, the NCAA slapped N.C. State with a two-year probation and declared the school ineligible for the 1990 NCAA Tournament. Although Valvano and his staff were found faultless in the investigation, the school later turned around and forced Valvano's resignation, effective at the end of the 1989–90 season. It was an inglorious end to his stay at N.C. State for Valvano, who in one sense felt vindicated by the NCAA investigation only to be thrown out into the cold by the school he had come to adore.

꘎

Charles "Lefty" Driesell was firmly established at Maryland when Valvano joined the ACC in 1980 as N.C. State coach, and Driesell admits he really knew nothing about the new coach in town:

At least I don't think I knew him at Iona. But I found him to be a great guy. He was a great guy to hang out with when we had coaching meetings in Myrtle Beach, and you know he was just a guy who was always having a good time. I also got to know him some from the trips we did with Nike.

A lot of coaches take coaching a bit too seriously, myself included. To him, it was more than just a game. He sometimes liked to play these crazy defenses against certain teams just to see what would happen. He'd do the same thing on offense, too. One time we were using a combination defense against him, and in response he took his two best players and put them in a corner to see what that would make us do. He liked to experiment, which I think made him a good coach. And he was inventive. He was fun to be around when he wasn't coaching, too.

I was more "old school" than Jimmy was. I remember one time when he was playing against a team with a big center—it might have been North Carolina, I'm not sure—and he put [five-foot-seven] Spud Webb on whomever the other team's center was while using a box and one. And he won. That's something I'd never do, but he made it work. He would do crazy stuff like that, whereas most other coaches are more fundamentally predisposed.

Yeah, he was a Yankee coach come South, but you couldn't dislike the guy because he was so funny. I got to know him a little bit better when I did some color commentary for the first two years after I left Maryland. I'd go out to dinner with him a few times and watch some of his practices, and so I got to know him a little better in that way.

❧

*When Valvano took the North Carolina State job, it meant a long move for the family in more ways than one, starting with the cultural change of going from the Big Apple to the laid-back South. **Pam Valvano** adapted quickly, but for Jim it was a move into a higher stratosphere of the college basketball world where the stakes and expectations were much higher:*

It was probably the easiest move I ever made. I loved it. Jim's parents would come and visit a lot. My brother was in Manhattan, but my mother was in Florida, so we had people all over the place.

I loved moving to North Carolina. I think it is a great

No, this isn't 1983 and the setting isn't Albuquerque, but Valvano is nonethe-
less enjoying the chance to cut down the nets. The occasion was Valvano's
first season at N.C. State and a championship-game victory over Saint John's
in the finals of the 1980 ECAC Holiday Festival tournament at Madison
Square Garden. (AP/Wide World Photos)

place to live. Jim was so great with the people, that they all loved him. He was a big dreamer and he knew if he wanted to win a national championship, he had to be in a school and a conference like this.

ভা

*In going to the ACC, Valvano was joining a conference where North Carolina's Dean Smith was, in essence, the dean of conference coaches, as **Lefty Driesell**, then the Maryland coach, recalls:*

Before Jimmy got to N.C. State, Norm Sloan, me, and some other conference coaches were always picking on Dean. And that's because he beat us all the time. If I remember right, when Jimmy got the job, he said, "Look, I want to be Dean Smith's friend. I'm going to be a competitor, but I'm not going to be—you know what I'm saying. He's not my enemy. I want him to be my friend and get along with him, and I want to beat him, too." That was a smart thing for him to say, being only about twenty miles from Chapel Hill. He wasn't worried about Dean; he wasn't threatened by Dean; he just wanted to coach his team and have fun and compete—something to that effect.

He *was* different. I heard that he once came to a game in a limousine and that sometimes he would take his staff out to eat when he was athletic director, and he was like the New York big-timer some people tried to make him out to be. I don't think he worried about spending money. It probably put him in the red at N.C. State. But that was just Jimmy, and I don't think he worried about anything much, which was good. It was an asset.

I was really upset the way N.C. State got rid of him and

handled his dismissal because I had gone through basically the same thing at Maryland. In some sense, I had a certain kinship with him because I knew him, and I think all coaches are close, even though we compete against each other. We have feelings for each other. And it was sad, and I knew Pam and I knew his children a little bit, because when I did games I'd see them. So it was sad to see him go that way. I know I sent him some telegrams and wrote him letters, and I told him I had him in my prayers.

❦

By going to the Atlantic Coast Conference in 1980, the young and exuberant Valvano was entering a different world defined by the buttoned-down countenances of the likes of Dean Smith at North Carolina and Terry Holland at Virginia. Life in the ACC would never again be quite the same, as **Alexander Wolff** *of* Sports Illustrated *recalls:*

One of the first things he did was get his own radio show. He wanted to introduce himself as something different, much like later on when Rick Pitino went to Lexington [to coach at Kentucky]. When Pitino first got there, people couldn't pronounce his name; they called him "Coach Patina." But Pitino was exotic. He opened an Italian restaurant and was perfectly comfortable being the outsider, being the New Yorker. And Valvano was like that, too.

He and Mike Krzyzewski got along because they had these ethnic sort of names, and they were young and they were dark. They both came from the Northeast, and we came to know both of them by single letters, V and K. But Valvano was a completely different breed from Krzyzewski. Coach K was kind of buttoned-down, where Valvano was much more of a free spirit. And I think Krzyzewski felt he sort of had to be that way, because to fit in at Duke you have to be formed in the Duke image. At N.C. State, on the other hand, they had to grope and come up with some alternative identity. And I remember Valvano talking about the times he fought the Carolina double standard. When one of their [North Carolina's] players got in trouble, no one ever heard about it. But if something happened on his campus involving one of his players, it was in the [Raleigh] *News and Observer* the next day.

He was really honest. I remember after N.C. State beat Houston a second time—the following season, after they had beaten Houston in the 1983 title game—afterward he said to me, off the record, something about how N.C. State shouldn't have been able to beat Houston because "We didn't have the talent," and that Houston was "the dumbest ____ing team in America." He was willing to be that honest. There was a certain generation of coaches that would never have confided that to a sports writer. He was very much a new breed.

⌀〰〰〰〰〰⌀

Dereck Whittenburg was already at N.C. State when Valvano arrived before the 1980–81 season, although they had already met:

I was recruited by Norm Sloan, but already knew Coach V. When I had been in high school [DeMatha High School, in Maryland], I played with a Washington, D.C., all-star team in the Boston Shootout at Boston University, and we had just won an overtime game against a New York team. I was out in the lobby area at the end of one court, sitting there with Sidney Lowe, who had also been my high school teammate. This guy came up to us and grabbed us around the neck like he was going to bang our heads together. It was Valvano. He looked at us and said, "I love you two guys, man, and I want you to come to Iona College. That's right; I own my own college. Come and play with us." We asked someone who this guy was and here he is a year later, our new coach at N.C. State.

When we found out that Valvano was going to be our new coach, I remembered who he was. I was just intrigued by his personality. Right off the bat he told us about how he was not only concerned with what kind of players we were, but what kind of people we were and what kind of students we were. He really wanted to know all about us. He would tell us about the dreams he had and would bring out the film from N.C. State's 1974 national championship year, and he instilled so much confidence in us. There was such a vision from Day One, and we bought into it. We decided we were going to follow this guy. It was about his message.

It was night and day from [Norm] Sloan. Sloan had been a tough, hard-nosed guy, even though he cared, and the personalities were so different, although Norm was good in his own way. Jimmy was smart in how he went about things in terms of how he kept things simple. He sold us on what our roles were, not by going around the room and asking us what our roles were, but in knowing what they were and relating that to us. I remember him coming to me and saying, "I want you to shoot the ball eighteen times a game and get me fifteen points a game," and I said, "Coach, I'm going to shoot the ball every time I get it and give you twenty points a game." He laughed, and that was a typical conversation in how he got you to think about what you were doing.

He wanted to know what we thought. Even in a huddle, he would ask us, "What do you think we ought to call, what should we play?" He made us a part of the leadership as well; he trusted us.

∽

Forward **Michael Warren** *was one of the five players in Valvano's first full recruiting class at N.C. State. He elaborates on the coach who had such a great influence on his life:*

V was a basketball genius, and people didn't give him a lot of credit for that. I had heard him on radio and seen him on TV, but I was bowled over by this guy the first time I met him. He starts talking and my mouth just drops open. I'm just sitting there and am immediately drawn into this guy. He's talking ninety miles an hour, and while I don't remember the details of what he was saying, I just knew that he was the most interesting coach I had ever met. With most other coaches, it was just a lot of coachspeak. With him, it was pretty damn impressive. He *dazzled* you.

He had on these old red nylon coaching pants and this white crumpled jacket, and it's obvious he certainly wasn't trying to impress me with his look. But he was a pretty impressive guy nonetheless. I was also being recruited by Bobby Cremins, who was then at Appalachian State [Boone, North Carolina], I liked him a lot, too, and my dad liked him a lot. He would come to town and spend a lot of time with my dad. . . . There was also Wake Forest. I talked to Duke some, and had also been in touch with some Ivy League schools such as Princeton and Harvard, as well as West Point. I didn't have any dreams of becoming the next David Thompson at N.C. State, but I thought this was great. I liked V and the players already there, so that's why I decided to go to N.C. State.

Once I got there, the thing I liked about him was that his structure was no structure. He knew in his mind what his structure was. There weren't any preseason drills, just a little bit of preseason conditioning in the form of running. The point was, he expected you to show up already in good shape on October 15 for the official start of practice. You had better be ready, was his philosophy. That's the same way he was about everything else, too. He always said he wanted to treat you the way he wanted to be treated—like an adult. In the end, near the end of his time at N.C. State, he ended up with some guys who couldn't handle that kind of responsibility, and that's ultimately what cost him.

After the '83 season, we started attracting more blue-chip players. I can remember one time walking through the Coliseum on my way to class and I see this recruit coming in to see the coaches. He looked to be about my size, and I remember thinking, *That SOB ain't going to take any of my playing time.* You know what? It was Len Bias [who eventually signed with Maryland and became one of the best players in the nation]. Well, as it turned out, he *didn't* get my playing time.

⚬⟶⟶⟶⟶⟶⟶⟶⟶⟵⟵⟵⟵⟵⟵⟵⟵⚬

Ray Martin, an assistant under Valvano for eight years, talks about that first year at N.C. State, which produced a 14–13 record:

It was a tough year. Like Jimmy said, that first year you're on a honeymoon: Everyone loves you, hugs you, and pats you on the back. You have a little time to build your program. What I remember most about that team is how much we played with passion, with enthusiasm, and all that came from Jimmy. He was the type of guy who could take any audience and have them eating out of the palms of his hands because he was a great speaker-motivator. Even when we had some tough losses during the season, Jimmy was able to keep the guys loose with what he said and how he acted toward them.

We hung in there and did a good job keeping everybody feeling good about themselves. It was a tough year, but then again when you worked for Jim Valvano, nothing seemed to be tough because he had a way of deflecting or diverting the negative onto himself and not onto his players. There's no question that players played their hearts out for him and they loved him.

It was kind of a culture shock for me being down South in an area without big cities, and I'm sure Jimmy felt the same way, because I was used to concrete and tall buildings. Plus you could play golf anywhere around there year round. There hadn't been a lot of places back in the borough of Queens where you could stick a tee into the ground, unless you could somehow push it through the concrete. But there are great people down there, and they welcomed Jimmy with open arms. That made the transition easier.

About a month and a half into the first year, we were getting ready to send out mailers to recruits. We had a decent brochure about our basketball program, but Jimmy asked me to collect brochures from other sports information directors to see how ours compared to the competition. I gathered the brochures from all the other ACC schools, brought them into Jimmy, and we lined them up on a table. Unfortunately, ours was probably the smallest and not the nicest compared to the other schools. At that, Jimmy said, "I'll be back," and he went down to the athletic director's office. Only Jimmy could do this. He sat down with athletic director Willis Casey and laid all the brochures on Mr. Casey's coffee table, and Mr. Casey put his eyeglasses down on his nose and, looking across the table at Jimmy, said, "Son, what can I do for you?" And Jimmy said, "Mr. Casey, I just want you to see these brochures so you can see what we're dealing with compared to all the others, and if we could just put a little more emphasis into building up our brochure, we would be able to compete better with Carolina and the other schools in the conference." Mr. Casey just looked Jimmy in the eye, then looked down at the brochures, gave a little grin, and said to Jim, "Let me ask you a question, Jimmy. If I gave you a brochure that looked just like the other ones in the conference, would you be able to guarantee me that we would win a national championship?" And Jimmy said, "Well, I don't know if I could *guarantee*, but I know that it would help." We eventually got a real classy brochure—after we won the national championship in 1983.

❧

Michael Warren, whose last season at N.C. State was 1983–84, recalls V's basketball practice habits:

He was a ball to play for. For instance, if we were supposed to start practice at four, we would stretch for ten or fifteen minutes just to get loose. Then we'd start shooting around, and after a while five o'clock would roll around and then 5:15, and all of a sudden the coaches would come in and say, "Okay, let's stretch for about five minutes, loosen up, and then we'll scrimmage." We practiced hard but only for about forty-five minutes, maybe a good hard solid hour. Then that was it.

We always practiced really hard the day before a game and then practiced light the day after, which was contrary to anything I'd ever done. He always felt if you went hard for a short period of time, it wasn't going to wear you out. In our preparation we would always scrimmage hard for about an hour, working on different things in the scrimmage. It was never any of this stuff where you break the practice down into all these little segments of time and then practice the same back-door play over and over. Talk about pure boredom—that would have been misery.

Practice would actually start around five o'clock or so and then we'd go hard until about six, and then we'd stop for a thirty-minute scouting report. For example, they would show us how Carolina sets up, and Jim V and [assistant] Ed McLean knew Carolina's offensive better than Carolina did. They knew everything. We just walked through it, and I might be pretending to be Michael Jordan and [Dereck] Whittenburg's guarding me, then they'd be jerking me around by the shirt saying, "This is where he's gonna go and this is where you need to go," and we'd do that for about thirty minutes. That left us only thirty minutes to shower and get to the dining hall before they closed down the food line at seven. Then, as soon as we were finished eating, it was back to the film room. Between 6:30 and 7:30, the coaches would have been up there, and what's amazing is how Ed McLean had been able to break down videotape in less than twenty-four hours from the last game so that it would be ready for the coaches to go over it with the players. He'd have every offensive cut on every offensive set spliced out right, and he knew where everything was on the tape.

During this hour when we showered and went to eat, the coaches would be up there sipping wine and smoking cigars. We would get up to the film room, which was pretty small, and by that time there would be a bit of a buzz up there. They'd be having a good time and it was a relaxed atmosphere. They were having a good time with this, and that's what basketball is all about. Having fun. It was really cramped in there, and everybody learned early that you didn't sit on the front row. When we got back there, everyone piled into the back because when V got excited going over the film, he'd start spitting all over you. Coach McLean would turn on the video, and V would highlight a few things, blah, blah, blah, and he'd be spitting. McLean would get into the video and he'd show maybe three minutes of a two-hour videotape, and V would grab the remote control and turn it off and say, "That's pretty much it. These guys are just going to go back-door on you every time, and if the ball goes here that's where it's gonna go, and this is what we need to do." And then he'd just get into his ranting and raving, pump 'em up, fire 'em up speech, and by then we're all tired and ready to go back to our dorm rooms. Some of us were going to do homework, some of us weren't, and that was it. And that was our scouting report.

I watch games now, and sit there seeing these players coming out of a time-out in just complete confusion, and I'm wondering what it is the coach has just told them to do. With V, it was just tell us something one time and that was it. I don't know what it was, maybe just a certain looseness or maybe it was simply that he recruited players who understood the game of basketball well and could quickly figure things out on their own. It was pretty impressive.

⟟⟟⟟

Warren remembers his first game as a college player, and it was in that game that he learned an important lesson—that Valvano, as fun and funny as he was, was quite serious about playing good basketball:

We were playing Campbell, and I was just thrilled to be playing. We were winning like 100–60, some ridiculous spread, and he decides to put all five of us freshmen in. We had a blast. It was no contest, and after the game we're downstairs in the locker room high-fiving and cutting up, and in comes Coach V. We were expecting him to say something like, "Hey, great first game and great way to start the year." But no. First thing he said was, "If I ever see you ____ing freshmen sitting on my ___damn bench laughing during the game, I'll run your asses out of here so fast it will make your heads spin!" All of a sudden, we're not in high school anymore. This was business. It was kind of a wakeup call.

Another time, I think it also was my freshman year, we were playing at Clemson. They were beating the crap out of us—it was about a twenty-point game at halftime. Well, V is just laying in to us, chewing us out, and he's ticked. He was standing right near one of those old, heavy-metal waste baskets like you used to see in grade school. I don't think he even knew it was metal because he suddenly kicked that thing, and it went flying across the room, and it hit Marty Fletcher, one of our assistant coaches, in the shin. Marty goes down to the floor, yelling and holding his shin. So I see this and so does [Walter] Dinky Proctor, one of my teammates and a really fun-loving guy. I looked over at Dinky and was trying to keep a straight face, and I could see that he was about to laugh. I'm thinking, *Oh, God, please don't laugh* as I put my head in my hands. Even in a serious time it was hilarious.

༄

Dereck Whittenburg, *who's now the head coach at Wagner College, quickly caught on to what made Valvano tick as an Xs and Os guy at N.C. State:*

He had a tremendous feel for the game and understanding opponents. His philosophy was to never let the best player on the other team beat you. So whatever we had to negate that, we did it. Like when we played Virginia and Ralph Sampson. It was a box and one, where one player was devoted to denying Sam the ball and everyone else played zone. It was all about percentages: He [Valvano] would say that the fewer times you let Ralph, or whomever the opposing team's star player is, touch the ball, the better chance you have of taking them out of their game and giving yourself a better chance to manage the game. If you can put more shooting attempts onto somebody else who isn't used to taking many shots to taking an extra five or six attempts a game, there's more of a chance that more of those five or six shots by the other guy would be missed. Percentages, that's what it is; taking shots away from the great player and putting them somewhere else.

⌒⧵⧵⧵⌒

As a former coach himself, television basketball commentator **Dick Vitale** *could appreciate what Valvano accomplished on the bench with teams that were, on paper, often overmatched by their opponents:*

Jimmy was the perfect example of a guy who really understood the flow of the game, the timing of the game, making the right substitution at the right time. I mean, his moves would be things that maybe were considered unorthodox or even something that you would be shocked with, but he knew how to bring in a particular kid at a certain point in the game to make a big play. He really understood how to manage the clock, how to manage the game, how to get the most out of people, and how to make certain that you can win with the strength of key people while understanding the weaknesses of people. He also knew how not to put players into a game in situations for which they weren't best suited. It all had to do with feel and instincts, and he was second to none. Jimmy had that special feeling and so did Al [McGuire]. I mean the two of them were New Yorkers, and I know they're up there [in heaven] sharing a lot of stories right now. They're probably having a blast. I bet right now they're battling over who gets to have Wilt Chamberlain on his team for the next pickup game.

⌀⍟⍟

Dereck Whittenburg will forever be a key link to that 1983 national championship season. He was the one who took the outside shot with the final seconds ticking away—a shot from about thirty feet that was falling short of the rim when forward Lorenzo Charles picked it out of the air to slam through for the winning basket over Houston as time ran out. Whittenburg recalls that incredible season and postseason tournament run:

Early on that season, we were like twelfth in the country, and Virginia and North Carolina were battling for one and two. At one point we were 7–2, and then I broke a bone in my foot while playing Virginia. Fifth metatarsal. I had done it twice before, once with each foot. After I went out, the team struggled a little bit, but then it regained itself, and then I came back against Virginia at Virginia. It was interesting because some of the younger guys, like Ernie Myers, got better after I had been taken out of the equation. They stepped up. Then when I came back, Jimmy told me, "You need to know that we've adjusted as a team in your absence, and it's up to you to fit back in with us, not the other way around." But he started me right away.

When we got to the ACC Tournament, Coach Valvano

told us that we probably needed to win at least one game in that tournament to get a bid to the NCAAs. We were 17–10 and a bubble team for sure. But here we were getting ready to play a first-round game against the very same team we had just blown out by about forty points to end the regular season—Wake Forest. We knew this wasn't going to be a forty-point game, but we ended up winning the game after Sidney [Lowe] made a nice late-game steal. In the locker room after the game, Coach V said, "Okay, this puts us in pretty good position, but if we win our next game, I think that will put us in for sure." Of course, our next game was "only" against North Carolina.

Then we won that game, and we all come into the locker room happy, and he says, "I guarantee you guys for sure, that if you win the next game, you're in." And, of course, that would mean winning the ACC Tournament and getting the automatic bid, although that's not what we were thinking. We never questioned what he was saying. When he would tell us stuff like that, we never went, "Oh, man, he's just fibbing us." We didn't even question him. We didn't even think about the third game of the ACC Tournament carrying an automatic bid with it, even though we laughed about it afterwards. We were so intent on what he was saying, like, "Okay, V, if that's what you want, let's go do it. *Boom*."

One thing that Jimmy did in selling us was that we talked about winning the national championship, and not just during tournament time. Where a lot of other coaches shied away from that kind of talk, we talked about it, and it was Jimmy leading us in the discussions. We talked about winning the ACC Tournament. We talked about going to the Final Four. We talked about winning the national championship. Jimmy fostered this kind of talk with us because he wanted to demystify for us the whole idea of winning the national title.

He figured the more we talked about it, the more realistic and attainable it would seem. That was consistent with his always saying that it was important to dream. If you can dream it and visualize it, you have a better chance of attaining it.

So when we were in a position to make all this stuff happen, it was nothing new to us. It was real to us. It was a plan. We talked about it. It was part of our everyday conversation. He made it a part of our thought process. We weren't intimidated by it, and it was incredible how focused we were.

Once the Wolfpack knocked off Virginia in the ACC finals— the third of four times those two teams would meet that season—it was then on to the NCAAs. **Whittenburg:**

Other than the Houston game in the championship contest, the most memorable game in the tournament as far as the team was concerned had to be the opening game against Pepperdine. We had to play the second overtime without Sidney Lowe, who had fouled out, and playing without him was like a football team not having its quarterback. I had played with him for three years in high school and now four years in college, and I was feeling a bit lost out there without him, like "Where's Sidney?"

We were down six points with twenty-five seconds to go, and the Pepperdine players on the bench were pointing at us and saying, "You go home now, ACC," and all that kind of stuff. I mean, they were talking a bit of trash, thinking they had the game won. But we came back and tied that game and then won it in overtime, and keep in mind there was no three-point shot. I remember that one of their best free-throw shooters missed two one-on-ones late in the game. Maybe what a lot of people didn't know about us is that we practiced a lot for game situations like that when there was less than a minute left and you had to know how to foul and how to use your time-outs. The NCAA changed its rules because of that.

The most memorable game in the NCAAs that year for me personally was the Virginia game [West Regional final]. I had a real good game, and I just had something for Virginia that year. I made free throws that put us ahead by one, and then they came down, but Othell Wilson missed a shot and Sampson put the ball back in, but it was after the buzzer. I was in front of the Virginia bench and kind of pointed at and taunted them a bit, but it was nothing vulgar or anything like that, and V didn't care.

⌒⌒⌒

There are two ways at looking at N.C. State's upset of Houston in the championship game of the 1983 NCAA Tournament. One, the more popular premise, is that this was the ultimate Cinderella story, that the Wolfpack didn't belong on the same court with the high-flying Phi Slamma Jamma gang of Houston. On the other hand, such a premise minimizes what N.C. State had done simply to get to the title game. No one plucked the Wolfpack out of nowhere and placed them in the final game; they got there by sweeping through the ACC Tournament and then by winning five straight NCAA Tournament games. Eight consecutive victories at that level and in that time of year is no fluke—the variables had worked themselves out and N.C. State was still standing. Sports Illustrated *college basketball writer* **Alexander Wolff** *takes a look back at the 1982–83 Wolfpack team and its amazing tournament run:*

I remember the team itself as a delicious collection of basketball personalities. I mean, you had these two chunky guards,

Dereck Whittenburg and Sidney Lowe, who could have been a couple of linebackers. Then in the frontcourt you had Thurl Bailey and Cozell McQueen, who were nice ballplayers but kind of skinny, especially McQueen. I remember McQueen, who's from South Carolina, delighting everybody in Albuquerque [at the 1983 Final Four] when somebody asked him why he had gone to N.C. State, and McQueen said, "I always wanted to go to school in the north." And, of course, there was [power forward] Lorenzo Charles, who we all remember for having taken that airball and turning it into a championship-winning basket. That last sequence was a summation of what Valvano stood for; you know, going from the ultimate downcast feeling to this almost impossible-to-conceive high. In a sense it was perfect. I mean, they didn't quit on the shot. It was Charles doing his penance for stealing the pizza off the pizza-delivery guy during the season by providing the head's-up play that wins the title.

⌒⌒⌒⌒

Michael Warren offers some tidbits about what happened during that magical late-season run in 1983:

We were rolling along pretty well that year until [Dereck] Whittenburg broke his foot against Virginia. We struggled, playing a little better than .500 ball for the rest of the regular season, but I do remember in that time how Ernie Myers, a freshman, stepped in and did a great job filling in for Dereck. He was practically unstoppable. . . . After we struggled most of February, we beat the crap out of [North] Carolina and then we beat Wake [Forest] in our last game of the regular season by something like forty points. Those two games are what really cranked it up for us.

Another thing I remember about all that is how little of school we saw in March. After we won the ACC Tournament in Atlanta, we returned to Raleigh on Sunday night and then turned right back around and headed out to Oregon for the first two rounds of the NCAAs. We beat Pepperdine and then beat UNLV, which was pretty hot at the time. The funny thing about that trip to Corvallis is that, I swear, the hotel we were staying in was a whorehouse. It was hilarious. I remember that Coach and Pam Valvano were staying in a room with a bed that was either heart-shaped or round with a red velour comforter, a mirrored ceiling, and a raised Jacuzzi. But this place was kind of a dump, too, even though the people there were great. I mean, what kind of hotel do you know that doesn't have a TV in the room, and yet has a love suite?

Then it was on to Ogden, Utah, where we beat Utah State and Virginia. Now things were starting to get pretty serious in terms of having a shot at the national title, but even then we were still pretty carefree. V was still the same. He hadn't changed in how he interacted with us or in how he prepared us for games. Even when on the road during the NCAAs, we would have film sessions in the hotels with the coaches sipping wine or whatever, just like they did back at Reynolds Coliseum during the regular season. V's whole deal, even back in February when we had been so inconsistent, was that, "Something good is going to come out of all this." Nobody had any real idea what that really meant because we probably weren't even the tenth-best team in the country at that time. But when we got back home from Utah knowing we would be going to the Final Four, it started to hit us, how unbelievable all this was. There were cars backed up out on the highway waving to us as we came in. We had five thousand people at our practices the few days we were back in town.

Throughout all this, you could see that V was just eating it all up. It was fun. We all were eating it up. What did we have to lose? And what did we have to prove? Nothing. And it really brought all of us together. There would be guys on the bus with a boom box with Lionel Ritchie songs cranked up, and everyone on that bus, including the doctors and the trainers, would be singing these songs at the top of their lungs. It was so much fun . . . touring the country on a bus and airplane with a bunch of guys that you liked. Here I was, nineteen years old, signing autographs for twelve-year-old girls, although after a while some of them were definitely older than twelve. And that's a whole other story.

When we got out to Albuquerque [for the Final Four], the temperature was in the seventies, and I can remember sitting by the pool. We were at a Ramada and actually got sunburned waiting to leave to go to practice. Then by Monday it was snowing. Think about it. On both days that N.C. State won the national title [in 1974 and 1983], it snowed in the city where the Final Four was being played—Albuquerque in 1983 and Greensboro [North Carolina] in 1974. That's pretty wild. When does it snow in April that far South?

✺

*Former Notre Dame guard **Ray Martin**, one of Valvano's first group of assistant coaches at North Carolina State, spent eight years in Raleigh and remembers N.C. State's 1983 West Regional final game against Virginia as one of the most unlikeliest of the six NCAA Tournament games that year because of the setting and the circumstances:*

We had just played Utah in the round before and had beaten them by almost twenty points, our easiest win of the tournament when we thought it might be one of the toughest, because, in effect, it had been a home game for them, with it being played in Ogden, Utah. And then we get Virginia for the regional final. It was our fourth game of the year against the Cavs, and what made it strange was that here was this matchup of ACC powers and it was taking place in Utah of all places.

Friends and players often kidded Valvano for his big nose and bad haircuts, and you can bet that he kidded them right back. (Courtesy of North Carolina State University athletics media relations office)

You've got to figure that they couldn't have been happier to play us because we had beaten them in the finals of the ACC Tournament. It was also Ralph Sampson's senior year, his last chance to win the NCAA Tournament. We knew it was going to be a tough game, but Jimmy had a way of keeping the guys motivated. He always kept the guys on their toes, always able to say the right things.

Each game was becoming more emotional and pressure-filled for us than the one before, and not only because of the way we were winning the games in the final minute. The momentum was building in more ways than one, because back then each game meant something like a hundred thousand dollars more for the school, and that's something that at least the coaching staff and administration were thinking about.

After we beat Virginia to win the West Regional and make it to the Final Four, you could see that Jimmy was experiencing the full spectrum of emotions. He was obviously drained physically and emotionally, in part because of the closeness of the games and in part because of reaching for new things to say to the guys to keep them up through all of this. The media part of all this was a factor, too. Jimmy had such a gift of gab. Add that to the fact that [Dereck] Whittenburg, [Sidney] Lowe and [Thurl] Bailey were very well versed in talking with the media, and we had what was becoming a sideshow. I'm not saying the media was hoping that we would win, but you could see the fun and excitement taking place in the media room after each of the victories. It was sort of like the *Tonight Show* every night. Jimmy was hosting it, and he would have everybody laughing. Each time out, as he would say, it was survive and advance. At the same time it was becoming very taxing.

꼬

Martin talks about what made that 1983 Wolfpack team so special:

The chemistry was perfect. We loved each other; we cared about each other. Jimmy cared about them and they cared about Jim, and it was just a magical ride. I think all of America was pulling for us. No question about it; we were the underdog and it showed in the reception that we received after winning the national championship and coming home to Reynolds Coliseum, which holds about twelve thousand people. I guarantee you there had to be about twenty thousand people packed in to welcome us back, and even the fire marshals might have been among the standing-room-only crowd.

One thing I will always be thankful and proud of is my being a part of two of the greatest moments in college basketball history. One was in 1974 when I was a freshman guard at Notre Dame and we scored the last twelve points of the game to beat UCLA, 71-70, to end their eighty-eight-game winning streak. That was incredible. Then to be a part of what happened with N.C. State in 1983. Those two moments will always rank high whenever some TV network puts together a highlights reel of great moments in college basketball history. What's ironic is that, to this day, I still have not seen the original tape of that last three and a half minutes against UCLA, during which we scored the last twelve points.

That 1983 season at N.C. State put us on a level where expectations became extremely high, and yet Jimmy always was able to let the players and the coaches understand who we were, where we were, and what it meant to represent North Carolina State and the state of North Carolina. So he kept a historical viewpoint in front of us all the time, starting with Wolfpack pride and what it meant to be at a school with a legacy that had included great coaches like Everett

Case and Norm Sloan's team of 1974 that included David
Thompson and those guys.

◦◦◦◦

*Pam Valvano recalls the 1983 NCAA Tournament
Championship run:*

It was incredible. First of all, Jim had a hernia at the time
and he was trying to be very careful to keep the thing from
rupturing so he wouldn't have to go get surgery. That was
kind of rough for him because he had to be careful about
jumping around during games and stuff like that. It could
have ruptured easily.

The last nine games of the season—through the ACC
Tournament and then the NCAAs—were miracles, every
single one of them. I went to every game, and was with him
in Albuquerque when he was sick as a dog. Not only did he
have the hernia problem, but he had also caught some kind
of flu bug where he had a 102-degree fever the night before
the Houston game. He had body aches, wheezing, and sweat-
ing. His dad would sit on the couch rubbing Jim's head and
putting cold compresses on him. He didn't know what to do,
and I'm there thinking, *Why did this have to happen? And how
are you supposed to be able to coach a team in the tournament
feeling like this? I don't know how you do it.* He was able to go
to practice; he wouldn't have missed practice for anything.
But I do remember watching the Houston-Louisville semifinal game on Saturday and thinking, *Omigosh, how's he going
to handle this?*

Afterward, the realization comes that you have just won
the championship—it was incredible. And even though it's
been so long since it happened, it will always be something

they can never take away from you. I'm glad in his lifetime he got to experience something like this. Some of this had to be luck, I hate to say it. Like the double-overtime game against Pepperdine. You think, *There's no way, no way, we're going to win*, and then we come back from the dead.

The funny thing about the Houston game was, LeeAnn, who was three at the time, was sitting on my lap during the game, and she had fallen asleep. At the end of the game—and this had turned out to be the case with all nine games through the postseason tournaments—if the game was close with two minutes to go, I would go through this ritual of getting up out of my seat, walking out of the arena, and going out into the hall with this pendant that was a gold wolf with red eyes. I would just sit there and hold this wolf and a bunch of others would gather around me and rub this wolf outside. Even if I forgot to get up to leave with two minutes left to go in a close game, fans would starting yelling at me, "Get out, Pam, get out!"

So, with two minutes to go in the Houston game, I'm out of there. I carried LeeAnn outside with me, and after I had been out there for what seemed like just a few moments, people were suddenly running all over the place. The game was over, and in the first few moments I didn't know who had won. I then walked back into the arena and there was everybody screaming and yelling, and I'm watching all this thinking, *Why aren't I down on the floor celebrating with everyone else?* That's one of the reasons Jimmy was running around on the floor not able to find somebody to hug.

✑

Alexander Wolff addresses the argument about whether N.C. State still deserved to be considered a decided underdog even after it made it all the way to the title game:

That comes from the fact that they barely got into the tournament. It was a small field, and I can't remember what seed they got, but their Cinderella story looks better than it probably really was because of the smaller field. And they were within seconds of losing at least once earlier in the tournament. So they were no juggernaut. But they had talent at every position.

They were a very good collection of guys for Valvano to play with. They were putty in his hands because he was very much a control coach and his guards were extensions of him, and they were able to do the whole systematic fouling thing when they were trailing to get the ball back and play two for one. So people who say it was a huge upset would look at N.C. State's shaky credentials in reaching the championship game, and then look at Houston and its incredible Phi Slamma Jamma cast.

From a distance, Houston looked plenty awesome, but if you look at the nitty-gritty a little more closely, it doesn't seem all that astonishing, particularly when you consider that in the college game of that era you could still systematically foul. Free-throw shooting was still really important, and I don't believe Houston had a good free-throw-shooting team. Furthermore, they were probably cocky after having beaten Louisville in the semis in what was basically a trapeze act with all the dunking, and then they looked over at N.C. State with its two chunky guards and the fact the Wolfpack had barely survived some close games, and Houston probably wasn't exactly quaking in their boots.

Valvano was so effective, particularly at that point in his

career, at being able to motivate his team and properly frame the moment. Who knows what he told them before they came out? But I'm sure he did an incredible job of it. It goes back to what he would do in recruiting these guys, things like having an N.C. State jersey with the kid's name on the back of it. He knew how to light the fuse. It wasn't beneath him to pull out all the emotional stops, and I think it was the kid in him that allowed him to relate so well to the kids who played for him. Valvano was still an adolescent in a lot of ways. The effectiveness might have worn off over time when he started to lose a little of his concentration coaching his team and went off into other things on his way to becoming a larger-than-life figure. But getting them focused for that one game in '83 was what he was really well equipped for.

⌒﹏﹏⌒

Michael Warren remembers some of the sights and sounds from the basketball court during the Final Four festivities in Albuquerque:

After we beat Georgia in the first semifinal on Saturday, I can remember we were dressed and coming back out. They had this real long, deep ramp on which you walked down into the Pit, and one of the funniest things I saw was right before Louisville and Houston were going to play. We walked right by the Houston guys who were all huddled up in their Phi Slamma Jamma shirts, and that's when I heard one of the stupidest things I've ever heard. Most teams, when they break a huddle like that, will put their hands together and yell something like "One, two, three, defense!" or say a prayer. But not these guys. Just before they break their huddle to bust out of the tunnel, they yell in unison, "We dunk better! Let's go get 'em!" Now, what the hell is that?

Well, we go out and we're watching this game, and these guys are unbelievable. I'm thinking, *You've gotta be kidding me!* You've also got to remember, though, that Albuquerque is pretty much at high altitude, something like five thousand feet, and those guys were sucking on oxygen. I remember our trainer telling us Monday night, "Okay, you guys, I'll give you oxygen if you need it, but don't just take this oxygen because it can do as much harm as it can good." I think Thurl may have chugged on it a couple of times, but overall none of our guys were using much of it. But Houston—they were sucking it down like water.

Going back to that Louisville-Houston semifinal game, I can remember Valvano telling the TV guys, "There's no way we would be able to play with these guys, that we would have to hold the ball, that the score might end up being 2–0, but there's no way we could run up and down with these guys. There's just no way we can do it. If we get the opening tap, we may hold the ball until halftime." V was really something. He was just setting those [Houston] guys up. And you've got to think that [Houston coach] Guy Lewis was no genius, anyway. I mean, how do you lose with that team?

Finally, we're in the locker room that night getting ready for the game. It's a scene I'll never forget. Just as he always did, assistant coach Ed McLean was up at the white board, dutifully diagramming stuff. This was where Coach V would usually step up and interject some comments between what Ed was saying. V might say, "Okay, Dereck, you've gotta do this," and "Sidney, you've gotta do that," and on and on. But this is the one time that you know Coach V had been dreaming about all his life, giving the pregame speech before the national championship game. This time, he comes to the front of the room and simply says, "If you think that we're gonna go out in front of sixty million people around the world and hold the ball and embarrass ourselves you're ____ing crazy! We're gonna go out there and shove it up their [butts]." And he was right. He and the coaches had the whole game broken down into four-minute segments to coincide with the TV time-outs, and in the first four minutes we were going to come out smoking. It worked. Oh, man, that group was so fired up that Jim could have taken the floor himself with two doctors and two trainers and taken on Houston. It was awesome. What I would give to have a videotape of that locker room scene.

Houston was always saying how the team with the most dunks wins. Well, the first points of the game were scored on a follow-up dunk by Thurl Bailey, and the last points were scored by Lorenzo Charles on a dunk. I'm pretty sure the only other dunk in the game was one by Akeem Olajuwon [of Houston], so when you think about it, Houston was prophetic: The team with the most dunks wins, and we out-dunked them, 2–1.

After Lorenzo made his dunk, it was just absolutely nuts. I can still see the clock ticking down the last three seconds off to the side while Lorenzo grabs the ball, dunks it, and then comes down with this little hop, and he just kind of looks around like, *What's next?* Lo had been one of my buddies from the day we walked on campus together, and I ran onto the court over to him, grabbed him around the neck, and said, "You did it! You did it! We won!" I can't remember my exact words, but I remember his exact words to me: "Let go my neck, man, I can't breathe!"

We didn't go to sleep that night. This was about the time that CNN was getting started, and I can remember it being three or four in the morning and CNN was showing videotape of scenes back in Raleigh of bonfires, and there we were half a country away watching this take place on our campus. It was unreal.

◊

*Assistant coach **Ray Martin** explains the mindset that Valvano was establishing with his team before they took the floor to play the Phi Slamma Jamma gang:*

Jimmy said there were two things that we could not do. The first was that we could not play afraid. That goes back to the game before when Houston had played Louisville and put on a jaw-dropping exhibition of dunk-it basketball. In fact, that may have been one of the greatest semifinals ever played in the NCAA Tournament. Both teams were flying above the rim the whole time. One of the things we did in preparing for the championship game against Houston was not show our guys film from that semifinal. In fact, after we had beaten Georgia in the first semifinal on Saturday, we sent the guys back to the hotel to rest. Yeah, they could still watch some of it on TV, but we knew it would be less of an impact than had they stayed behind to watch the game in person.

The coaches stayed and watched the first half, and we see these guys flying all over the place dunking and all that stuff. When we got back to the hotel, we went to Jimmy and Pam's room, and there's Jimmy lying in bed, sick with a 102-degree fever. Even our team doctor was in there, tending to Jimmy, although he had his TV on, of course, watching the game. He asked us coaches to come in and we all decided it would be best to not show the tape of the Houston-Louisville game to our players in preparing for the championship game.

The second point he made in the pregame speech was to tell the guys to make sure that Houston never dunked the ball. No dunks, period. And that's pretty much what happened—they might have had one dunk, I'm not sure—but the irony is that we scored our first basket of the game on a dunk and then our last basket of the game on a dunk—with Lorenzo Charles slamming off of Dereck's long shot.

In essence, Jim's message for that game was "Play your butts off, guys, but be loose." Of course, he had a whole different spin for the media, as in "Oh, we're so lucky to be here, and what are we going to do trying to guard these Phi Slamma Jamma guys?" So he got quoted saying stuff like that in the papers prior to the game, and then he was able to turn around and use that as motivation for his players. He was a master motivator. A master motivator! You know, he would use anything and everything that he thought would hit home with his guys. But again, we were a special group of people, and I think any team that wins a national championship is made up of special people.

☙∞❧

Martin offers his take on the Houston game:

There were a couple of key points in the game. One was when Clyde Drexler picked up his second foul with still a lot of time to go in the first half, and for some reason Guy Lewis kept him in the game. Then with about five minutes left in the half, Drexler was coming down on a fast break, a two on one, and there was Terry Gannon, our sixth man, a great shooter, back alone playing defense and doing what he could to keep them from getting the easy basket. Terry sacrificed his body and took the charge from Drexler. We get the foul and now, suddenly, Drexler has three fouls and the first half isn't even over yet. That was a key point because, obviously,

Drexler was one of their big weapons, and for all practical purposes he had now been neutralized. At least, he couldn't be as aggressive anymore as he usually was. That made him sit down. Finally.

The second key point came midway through the second half after Houston had gone on a 17–2 run to take the lead on us. All of a sudden, Coach Lewis decides to take the air out of the ball and slow it down, apparently content to sit on the lead and milk the clock down. So there's [Akeem] Olajuwon, Drexler, [Michael] Young, and all those guys who had just put together one of their patented runs doing our work for us—slowing things down, because we had always said in preparing for them to not let them get to the point where they were making six or eight runs down the court. Even then, we didn't have any way of stopping them, no matter what we tried, and then they simply stopped and slowed things down. We couldn't have designed it any better.

As we started getting our second wind and coming back at them, we could see that they were getting a little tight. We were chipping away at their lead and the clock was running down, and that was our type of game. It had been for the whole postseason, both in the ACC Tournament and now in the NCAAs. I think they were shocked, especially when Dereck Whittenburg hit two or three outside shots in succession.

Sidney Lowe, to me, was one of the finest point guards ever to play college basketball. He was coming down and weaving through traffic, weaving through defenders, and he was looking for Dereck, who was lined up eighteen to twenty-five feet from the basket to knock them down, and then Terry Gannon hit a jump shot and the next thing you know it's a two-point game. For us, it was familiar territory—our comfort zone. We felt very confident, and Jimmy believed that it was our game to win. He always felt this was going to be our game to win.

⌾

Sidney Lowe, former N.C. State player:

The Houston team walked in, wearing sunglasses, listening to their Walkmans, and with their slippers on—like they were going to the beach or something. Me and Dereck [Whittenburg] were there looking at each other and getting kind of angry about it. Us and Terry Gannon, who at five-ten would fight anybody or anything at the drop of a hat if he felt like he needed to. We all got fired up about that thing. We felt right then and there that we could beat them if we played our game.

When Dereck and I watched them beat Louisville in the semis, we had some doubts ourselves. . . . But that was the day before they came strolling into the shootaround with their slippers on. It was clear to us that they felt they had already won the national title. They weren't even thinking about us. No one had to say a word to us. Dereck and I were fired up just looking over there at them. Here we were dripping with sweat because we had just finished a pretty good workout. And then these guys come in like they didn't have any work to do. It just [ticked] us off.[1]

⌾

Dereck Whittenburg talks about the Houston game and the premise of N.C. State as underdog:

Before the game Jimmy was giving this speech about how we

belonged here and now we can go out and win it, when all of a sudden Phil Spence from the 1974 championship team blows in through the locker room door and says, "We're the Wolfpack, and we can do this, and we're going to win the national championship!" and that's how we broke out. *Boom!* We were ready to go, and ran straight out to begin our warm-ups. That was incredible.

We were up at halftime, and we were so focused on the result of the game, like we were in a zone and were so used to winning that Coach V never ever thought we were going to lose, and that goes back to the Pepperdine game in the first round while going so long without Sidney. We never blinked. We got to a point after the NCAA Tournament, a subconscious thing, that we got so used to believing we just kept going. "Okay, whatta we gotta do to win this game?" Even at halftime of the Houston game, there was no big rah-rah. It was just, "This is what we've got to do, now let's go out and do it."

I think he truly knew us as people. He knew what we thought. He knew us as individuals. It wasn't a matter of his pushing a button. It was more like he had the remote controls to us, and there's a difference. Everyone talks about how great Houston was and how incredible Phi Slamma Jamma was, but that didn't really affect us that much. Remember, we had already played North Carolina and Virginia a total of seven times that year, and they were clearly two of the best teams in the country. Against Houston, we didn't blink. We had played against the best in the ACC, and we knew we were good.

I don't know how the tempo got the way it did [fairly slow], but they were more athletic than us, and we knew we had to dictate the tempo to have a better chance to win. I think they thought they were going to play us any kind of way and just beat us. I don't think they thought about tempo or even cared about tempo. They didn't do anything to dictate any kind of style.

I can still visualize that last time-out with under a minute left. I can see [assistant coach] Tom Abatemarco twisting at his moustache, and I remember thinking, *Just get me the ball,* and *I want the shot.* The game was tied. We called a five-play that sets me up for a one-on-one while looking for Thurl coming off a double screen because we were anticipating a man-to-man, but they ended up coming out in a 1-3-1 trap. We were looking for Thurl because we figured [Akeem] Olajuwon wasn't going to come out. Because of the trap, we had to spread out and pass the ball around. We just kind of reacted and weren't worried about turning the ball over. We knew the clock was winding down. Sidney threw the ball to Thurl in the left corner and I'm over in the middle. Olajuwon came out on Thurl, who is now stuck holding the ball and saw me. He threw it, and it almost got stolen. I had to reach back with both hands to get it and I knew it was time, that I had to get it up in the air. I'm thinking, *I'm going to make it,* and it really wasn't that far away. He [Charles] caught it right by the rim, and the rest is history. Great alley-oop pass, huh?

❦

At that point, pandemonium broke out. **Whittenburg** *describes the moment and the long-term aftermath:*

It's just like in baseball when the guy hits the home run on the last pitch of the game and everyone piles on him after crossing home plate.

Whenever I go back to North Carolina, there are people

who come up to me wherever I go to tell me where they were watching the game and what they were doing when we scored that winning shot at the end.

⟨∾∾∾⟩

Michael Warren, who still lives in Raleigh, recalls what Valvano told his team after they had beaten Houston to win the national championship:

None of those fifteen guys' or three or four coaches' lives were ever the same after that. It's been almost twenty years and to this day I can't go anywhere around here without people recognizing me and the national championship ring I wear and stopping me to talk about that season of '83. Coach V told us, "You guys don't even understand it yet, how big an accomplishment this is for you and what it will mean ten, fifteen, or twenty years from now. It will grow bigger, and bigger, and bigger." And he was right. I think everybody affiliated with that team has been successful in whatever they chose to do, regardless of whether or not they have a college degree.

⟨∾∾∾⟩

*As good a friends as Valvano and **Dick Vitale** were, their friendship sometimes got put to the test when Vitale worked a network telecast of North Carolina State games, such as one time when the Wolfpack was beating up on nemesis North Carolina while Vitale was touting the virtues of Tar Heels coach Dean Smith:*

North Carolina State was pounding Carolina, just pounding them. V's just blowing them out like you can't believe, and he's in control. Near the end, during the last three minutes of the game, I'm saying over the air, "Well, this is North Carolina and this is Michelangelo—Dean Smith—and Dean Smith's got a history of pulling miracles and getting teams to come from behind," and so on and so forth. Well, the next morning, I mean it must have been seven o'clock, maybe seven-thirty in the morning, I get a phone call at the hotel, where I'm getting up and getting ready to go to the airport, and it's Jimmy. He starts calling me all this stuff over the phone and gets on my case about my having talked so much about Dean Smith in those last few minutes when it was N.C. State that was getting it done. He says, "You're an Italian, but what do you know about being an Italian?" and he proceeded to bust my chops. He says, "There we were pounding North Carolina and I never heard one thing about Jimmy V doing his job. Instead, it's all about this miracle Michelangelo guy being so great." But he was saying all this stuff in a good-natured way, laughing and fooling around with me.

He had such a great sense of humor and just loved being on stage or as a commentator with the red light on him. But he was such a good guy as well. And then he got himself into a situation—and we talked about this so many times—where he became a victim of sorts because of the pressures of trying to survive in big-time college basketball and staying on top of the ladder, where you'd maybe bend your admission standards to get a particular kid into your program so you could stay competitive with blue-chip players. Then when the book [*Personal Fouls* by Peter Golenbock, a blanket indictment of Valvano's perceived handling of the N.C. State program] came out, he was so crushed. I'm not saying there was no validity at all to the book, but Jimmy felt the book centered on nothing more than the negatives and never with the players who loved him and understood what he was about and really were in his corner.

Obviously, whenever you are at that level, you're going to have players that will be a little unhappy. But where he made a mistake was in pushing the button to want to win like anybody else wants to win: You start taking chances on too many kids with borderline academic backgrounds. And when you start doing that, it comes back a hardship, especially if you don't win big and you're being compared all the time with Duke and North Carolina in terms of graduation rates and those kinds of things. And that just kept eating at him, and he would always make the point about graduation, "Well, how come they don't include my graduation rate at Johns Hopkins? Every kid there graduated that I coached." But even Jimmy would admit at the end that he started making a mistake on a couple of kids. Taking a chance on one or two is fine, but going beyond that can mean trouble.

In defense of Jimmy, take a Chris Washburn. Everybody later could look back on that in hindsight and say, "Oh, wow, major mistake, taking a chance on a kid like Washburn who had no grades academically coming out of school." It was documented how he really struggled on the tests and all that stuff. The real point in all that was that what had happened was that Jimmy had only done a better job of recruiting Chris Washburn than anybody else because Chris could have gone to almost any school in America. He would have had a limousine waiting for him at the airport as soon as he got off the plane anywhere he wanted to go. It was a good final argument in Jimmy's behalf that he had just been better than everyone else in recruiting Washburn in a situation where there is pressure everywhere to survive, and not everybody is going to be able to get the student who combines great basketball and great grades. Yet you get your alums and all your people around you wanting you to beat people who take players like that all the time. Sometimes to beat them you've got to load the dice and gamble like heck.

Jimmy came from a background where he always believed if you gave somebody an opportunity, you never know what good might come of it. His argument is that we live in a country where we give people chances, and he wasn't going to turn his back on giving somebody an opportunity. Still, he knew it might come back to bite him and, unfortunately, in a couple of cases it did. But talk to people who knew him or coached with him or played for him, guys like [Dereck] Whittenburg and [Sidney] Lowe, and you get a good picture of how much Jimmy really wanted to help people. There was one player, for instance, who was given an opportunity by Jimmy when no other coach wanted to give him a chance. Actually, he was doing a favor for a friend of Rocco's, his father. And Jimmy took this kid and just worked with him and worked with him until he became a pro, a standout in the NBA.

Jimmy had a passion for working with people, for making them better. He loved going to the summer camps and talking to the kids. What he didn't really love was the everyday practice situation. He really didn't. That part of the gig didn't excite him as much. I know he loved television. When he got on the TV he loved it, but I think down deep he was hoping something would break [career-wise] when it came to analyzing and talking basketball because that was something he loved and had a knack for. Then he gets something good going, only to pass away at such a young age. I really believe that something might have happened for him in the way of entertainment because he had a special presence in front of the camera. He was Seinfeld before Seinfeld.

❦

Behind all the jokes, big smiles, jumping and running around, there was a side to Valvano that people who didn't know him well couldn't have known about or at least wouldn't have suspected based on superficial examination. And that was that Valvano was a deeply sensitive and contemplative man, as Charlotte Observer *sports reporter* **Charles Chandler** *points out:*

It's almost like you didn't have him pegged as the greatest Xs and Os guy but that he can recruit and he's all over the place and his hair is flopping around. Still, there was a sense that there was a lot more to Jim than he's telling us—a whole lot of depth there. Something told me that he was a guy who could outsmart you, and you might not know you're being outsmarted.

Those days when he was coaching at North Carolina State were, to me, the real glory days of the ACC. That will probably go down as the golden era in the ACC. Jim's role was as kind of a fun disrupter. He just had his own deal, a different one.

⁓

Chandler *had been working in the paper's Raleigh bureau covering the Wolfpack in the late eighties, around the time that Valvano's world at N.C. State was starting to fall apart:*

There had been times before my last interview I did with Valvano, when he was dying of cancer, that I would be sitting in his office with him and his attorney, Art Kaminsky. Because the *Observer* was not the Raleigh paper, we probably were perceived by Jim as being a little friendlier to his cause, although we were all going after the same story and we all had to report what we found to be true. Still, we had a good relationship even in the midst of what was going on.

There were times after games or whatever that I'd be in his office with him and Kaminsky and others, and he'd kind of get his cigar going and be funny, yet he would express his frustration and sadness. I think what he felt was the injustice of how things were being spread around about him and the program. The difference from seven years earlier was so pronounced. I wasn't covering him then, but I along with everybody else was watching it when he won the championship in '83. And then you get to the place where you're covering him in the midst of this controversy, which was kind of a professional flaw of sorts; whether it was deserved or not, it was. Then to be there when he was dying, it's just—I don't know. I was thirty-three at the time when I did that last interview with him, and it really did a number on me.

I tried to write the story. I felt like it was my professional obligation not to let anything that I was feeling influence what came out in the paper. This thing needed to be written as pure as it could be. But in terms of what was going on and the emotions of it—that was a time where I just had a hard time detaching myself from it.

❧

Valvano spent seven more seasons at N.C. State following the 1983 championship season, and while he didn't win any more titles with the Wolfpack, several of his teams went deep into the NCAA Tournament. His 1984–85 and 1985–86 teams both made it to the Elite Eight: In 1985 the Wolfpack lost to Saint John's, 69–60, in the West Regional Final; and in 1986 they lost to Kansas, 75–67, in the Midwest Regional Final played in the Jayhawks' backyard—Kemper Arena in Kansas City, Missouri. Guard **Vinny Del Negro**, *still active in the NBA as of 2001, was a member of both of those teams:*

The loss to Kansas was really tough because we were up by seven with about four minutes left in the game at Kemper Arena. But then their fans started that chant of "Rock, chalk, Jayhawk!" over and over, and I guess it psyched us out because we lost our composure and lost the game.

We had some really good teams during the years in the mid-eighties. We were deep in talent with guys like Lorenzo Charles, Spud Webb, Nate McMillan, Ernie Myers, and Chris Washburn who played some in between those times in which he got in some sort of trouble. I was able to play alongside some real characters in those days, even though I didn't play much my first two years, in part because we were so deep. Spud was a phenomenal athlete and Nate was a good rebounding guard who could also handle the ball real well.

V changed the whole complexion of N.C. State because of who he was. His recruiting flourished after his 1983 team won the championship, and he had a lot to do with that. He was incredible just in terms of his intelligence alone. This was a guy who would recite poetry to us and yet he was so genuinely fun loving. He also bonded so well with us. I remember going to visit him in his office, and he would be sitting in his chair smoking a cigar while munching on microwaved popcorn. And he loved eating that popcorn. While he was very serious about being a basketball coach and was so competitive about it, he was able to stay loose and he kept us loose. That was his demeanor. He wore his emotions on his face: He would look at you and you could pretty much tell what he was thinking before he said it. He would not only be straightforward and honest in communicating things to you, he also was a great listener. It's no wonder people gravitated toward him, and in part that's because he liked to have fun, too.

As Wolfpack coach, Valvano stayed as close to the action as he could, meaning he never stayed seated on the team bench much during games.

(Courtesy of North Carolina State University athletics media relations office)

Del Negro goes into more detail describing Valvano as a recruiter and his passion for the game:

I remember his coming to recruit me. One of the other schools I was being recruited by was Kentucky. Joe B. Hall [Kentucky's head coach at the time] and assistant Leonard Hamilton came to my house dressed up real formally in these nice suits, and then a week later Coach V and assistant Tom Abatemarco came to my house loose and relaxed in these Nike warm-ups. It wasn't long before they were wrestling around in our living room, and I felt so comfortable in their presence. This was no act; they were just enjoying themselves, and within a week I signed my letter of intent with N.C. State.

One thing that helped me bond with Coach V was that we both came from Italian families, where family is very important. And he was so passionate about things, especially basketball. Yeah, he took it very seriously. I remember one time, I think it was my senior year when we were playing at Virginia, there were only about four or five seconds left in the game when I got fouled. I don't remember if the score was tied or if we were up by one, but I got fouled and he called a time-out. The place was really loud and we lost track of time during the time-out, taking too long. By the time we came out of the huddle, the ref had already placed the ball on the free-throw line and was counting down the seconds. We rushed out there, I grabbed the ball and quickly shot it, but two of our guys taking position were still in the foul lane when I released the ball, and we were called for a violation. Virginia got the ball back, drove the length of the court, and one of their guys made a running one-hander as time ran out to beat us. Going to the bus after the game, I spotted Coach V off to the side crying his eyes out because of the way we had lost the game. That's the sort of passion he had for basketball.

Another time, in 1987, we were playing in the Rainbow Classic in Hawaii, where we won the championship by beating Creighton, Louisville, and Arizona State. I don't remember which of those games it was, either Louisville or Arizona State, I guess, and we were trailing at the half. Coach V was livid. He came into the locker room and just started ranting and raving at us, and it was like he was about to lose it, he was so angry. At one point, he reached out and slammed the locker room door behind him, just at the time when our team doctor Dr. Manley, who was about sixty years old, was walking in through the door. But Coach V didn't see him, and when he slammed the door, it smacked Dr. Manley and knocked him to the floor. He was out cold, and just like that the room went deathly quiet. Fortunately, Dr. Manley was okay and he eventually got back up. Only then did Coach V start laughing in obvious relief, realizing what he had done and how silly it was of him to do that. Pretty soon everyone was laughing, and we went back out and took control of the game.

As a coach, he was always willing to try different things, looking to throw the other team off their game. He used a lot of trick defenses. He would switch from a box-and-one to a triangle-and-two to a one-three-one zone to a fullcourt trap to a fullcourt press and then switch his zone defenses around. He kept our practices interesting as well. We could be just loosening up with stretches or calisthenics at the beginning of practice, and he would be walking among us, suddenly stepping in front of one of us and taking a charge, falling back onto the floor. Yeah, basketball was serious to him, but he had fun with it, too.

∽᠊᠊᠊

*One of Valvano's last star players he coached at North Carolina State before leaving there in 1990 was point guard **Chris Corchiani**, who had been recruited by Valvano and spent his first three years with the Wolfpack playing under Valvano. Corchiani became the first player in NCAA Division I history to hand out at least one thousand assists as a collegian, and twice he led the ACC in assists. He remembers what it was like being recruited by Valvano:*

I knew right away from the very first time I met him that he was somebody special. He had the kind of personality where he was a magnet to people—people just liked being around him and they were drawn to him.

Within fifteen minutes of the time that he and assistant coach Dick Stewart came to visit me at my house, Coach V was rearranging the furniture in our living room while giving me and my parents a breakdown of the North Carolina State system of offense and defense. The sofa was the big man in the middle and the TV set was the outside shooter, and by the time he got done with all this the entire living room had been rearranged. It was really something to see. It was simply amazing how he did it, and he made it really easy to follow what he was demonstrating.

He stayed at our house until the wee hours of the morning. I can remember after midnight we went outside to play basketball in the driveway, where we had a goal set up and a light out there so that we could play. We ended up playing a game called TAPs, where you take only three-point shots, and if you miss, a player from the other team can tap the rebound in and get credit for a basket if he touches the ball before it hits the ground. It was Coach Valvano and Coach Stewart against me and my dad, and what struck me was how competitive Coach V was, even playing a game like that so early in the morning. He never stopped talking the whole time we were playing, and it was a blast.

The thing about Coach V is that he was continual motion and nonstop noise. He was never quiet. There have been people over the years who have tried to emulate his personality, but there's nobody who could be just like him, first of all because they couldn't keep it up all the time like he did because that's who he really was. He was someone who could walk into a room full of people, and everyone would stop what they were doing or saying so they could listen to him. E. F. Hutton had nothing on him.

ᨆᨆᨆ

Corchiani was a junior during the 1989–90 season, which was Valvano's tenth and final season as the Wolfpack coach. It was a last-hurrah season at N.C. State for Valvano, whose team was playing under the dark cloud of an NCAA investigation coupled with a school administration at odds with Valvano. Valvano ended up losing his job over what was later determined to be minor NCAA infractions, but the attack on his character had caused harm that, while not irreparable, put a damper on what he and his teams had accomplished during those ten seasons. Corchiani recalls that 1989–90 season, which was his next-to-last in a Wolfpack uniform:

Nineteen ninety was a tough time for him, and I know it affected him greatly. But he was one of those guys who would never let you know what he was really feeling. Still, as bad as that year had to be for him, it was my most memorable year of the four I played at N.C. State. He would keep saying, "Hey, guys, it's us against the world, and I need a few good men to help get us to where we need to be going. Everyone

Valvano vents in the final moments of N.C. State's 69–61 loss to Georgetown in the 1989 NCAA Tournament's Round of Sixteen. It turned out to be Valvano's last appearance as a coach in the Big Dance. (AP/Wide World Photos)

wants us to fail, but I'm not going to let that happen, and I need all of you to chip in and help out. We're going to be strong, and that's because we're going to work together."

There was so much negative stuff coming out in the media at the time, and that's what made it so refreshing that year being around him and being with the team. I remember him telling us how every day he couldn't wait to get to the gym or to get to the locker room because those were the only places he could go and get way from all the horrible stuff going on around him.

In our last game of the season, we played Wake Forest and were down by something like fifteen or twenty points late in the game when he called a time-out with about thirty seconds left. He called the time-out so he could call us together one more time and thank us for hanging with him that season and tell us how great a year it had been for him. That was a classic move. It was an incredible way of thanking us in a setting where it meant so much to us.

He was a genius, and I think in some way he was one step ahead of the administration in all this. You've got to remember that almost everything with him was a game, and this whole thing with the NCAA and the administration might have been no different. In fact, I think there was a part of him deep down inside that liked what was happening because it presented another challenge to him, a challenge that he could rise up for and beat with a plan. Whatever it was, he kept fighting and working as hard as ever throughout the season.

ᏯᎷᎷᎯᏉ

Bill Foster, *Valvano's coach at Rutgers, was among the many basketball fans on hand in February 1993 when N.C. State*

*brought the 1983 Wolfpack team together to honor Valvano and
his players before a game that day with Duke:*

Brent Musberger was there doing all of the introductions of the
players, assistant coaches, and managers of that 1983 team, and
then it got to the end when it was time to introduce Jimmy.
I'm sure he was tired and who knows how much pain he was in,
and when Jimmy got the mike after being introduced [by N.C.
State football coach Dick Sheridan], he was unbelievable. He
more than came to life. I'll never forget that day.

That night he invited several of us over to his home, and
we sat around and laughed as Jimmy told stories. And with
Jimmy, you just listened; you didn't want to butt in. Then
he got tired around 8:30 or 9:00, and we knew by then it was
time to leave so that he could get his rest.

I also went with him one time to the cancer center in
New York when he went in there for a treatment, chemo I
think. There was a group of people in the room with Jimmy,
other cancer patients, and Jimmy had them all forgetting
their own problems. He had them laughing and was telling
them stories. It was a touching thing for me to watch as he
dug so deep in sucking it up and keeping going.

Last year [2000], I went down to visit Dick Vitale at his
house and we got to talking about Jimmy. And I told him,
"You know, Dick, it seems like he's still here." That speaks
of the effect that he had on myself, and Dick said he felt the
same way. That tells you how powerful a personality he was.

⌒⟶

Nick Valvano *talks about his brother's ten-year tenure at N.C.
State and how it helped him out in his own work as a businessman:*

Just to see him get to be in the top echelon of his profession was very moving to me. I'm very proud of him. He was so approachable. When I was entertaining customers down in North Carolina, I would give Jim a call and see if he was free to come over and have dinner with me and my clients. He just enjoyed people. He would come and sit down at the table with us, eat off someone else's plate, make fun of me—just a funny guy, and everyone loved him. They loved the attention.

His years at State were special because he had reached the top of his profession. I try not to be biased—yeah, he made some mistakes, but the punishment was worse than the crimes committed. To his credit, last year the N.C. State board of trustees passed a resolution that recognizes Jim's accomplishments both in terms of what he did at N.C. State and for his contributions. This has actually been described as a "healing resolution." It was driven by a few of the retiring board members who had been supporters of Jim and felt that the whole situation leading to his resignation had gotten out of hand. They wanted to do something to recognize that that was a small part of Jimmy's life at N.C. State. It was not a necessary thing, but it made a lot of people feel good. That's the way it should be. Jim absolutely loved N.C. State.

❦

Dave Didion, the NCAA's lead investigator of the N.C. State case, wrote a revealing letter to Valvano after the investigation was complete:

I wanted to let him know that he had cooperated with me more than any coach I had ever worked with, and that not everyone thought he was evil. I wanted to let him know that if I had a son who was a prospect, I would be proud to have him play for Jim Valvano. He wasn't the smart-ass egomaniac I'd anticipated. Yes, the graduation rate of his players was not good . . . but no one cared to look at the overall graduation rate at N.C. State. Yes, he probably shouldn't have recruited some of the kids he did. But if he hadn't, he'd have ended up playing against them and getting his brains beaten out by them because everybody else wanted those same kids.[2]

3

JIMMY V VS. THE BIG C

The diagnosis came down in June 1992, a little more than two years after Valvano had ended his coaching regime at N.C. State. For months leading up to the diagnosis, Valvano had been suffering from a mysterious back pain, particularly aggravating during the long stretches he was seated doing basketball commentary for ABC and ESPN. When x-rays showed that Coach V had cancer, or more specifically metastatic adenocarcinoma, his first reaction to the doctor pointing out the dark spots on the film was that the x-ray technician had neglected to use a flashbulb. He wasn't trying to get guffaws; it was more of a funnyman's serious way of dealing with the shock.

For the last ten months of his life, leading up to his death on April 28, 1993, Valvano gallantly soldiered on. Despite being wracked with pain and often nauseated from his chemo treatments, Valvano kept working as a television commentator almost to the end. He often flew to the ESPN studios in Bristol, Connecticut, where he not only fulfilled his commitment to analyze college basketball, but did so with his usual flair and energy. Even though he was seriously ill, Valvano showed his brightest side to millions who knew he had cancer but didn't think about it much because he looked and sounded so good. Cancer, schmancer.

Two unforgettable moments in the last three months of Valvano's life live on as testaments of what it means to really live. One was his appearance in February 1993 before a Duke–N.C. State game at Reynolds Coliseum for a tenth-anniversary celebration of the 1983 championship team; the second his thirty-minute speech in March 1993 at ESPN's American Sports Awards show, otherwise known as the ESPYs. In both cases, Valvano could barely walk to his appointed round, yet he subsequently delivered fully charged inspirational speeches that remain as memorable as his celebratory running and jumping following the 1983 victory over Houston. Even in private Valvano touched people's lives, frequently being the one who would cheer up other cancer patients awaiting treatments in the catacombs of some hospital.

In the last year of his life, Valvano teamed up with ESPN to create the V Foundation, a nonprofit company raising money for cancer research and awareness. Valvano's legacy lives on in many ways. Cancer beat Valvano. Or did it?

Terry Gannon, *one of Valvano's players at N.C. State and now a network TV sportscaster, was about to broadcast a base-ball game when he got the news that his mentor and good friend had cancer:*

I was getting ready to broadcast a game for the Charlotte Knights, a Triple-A club for the Cleveland Indians. I was back in the media dining room eating a pregame meal and watching [ESPN] SportsCenter when they announced that

Coach V had cancer. I went straight home to Raleigh without broadcasting the game, and by the time I got home there must have been thirty-five phone messages for me on the recorder from everyone from friends to reporters wanting to talk to me to see how I felt.

I had last spoken to V about a week earlier, and I knew then that he hadn't been feeling well, that he had been suffering from back pain for a while. The real shock for me in all this wasn't in finding out that a friend had cancer; it was in finding out that V had cancer. I just couldn't believe that a man so full of life and so relatively young now had a life-threatening disease.

I saw him within a couple of days after getting back to Raleigh. When I saw him, I remember how we hugged each other and didn't just laugh it off. We talked very seriously about cancer. One thing Coach V had always taught me was that it's okay to let your emotions out, to not hold anything back. Most people knew him for his public persona of being upbeat and quick with quips, but people who knew him well knew that he had no qualms about showing his emotions. It was okay to cry. The other thing he taught me is that, "Somebody has to do it, so why not me?" Step up to the plate. "You wanna do college football play-by-play? Somebody has to do it—why not me?"

At first after he learned he had cancer, he did very well. We played golf a couple of times, and I was surprised by how well he was playing considering that he was getting medical treatments such as chemo and radiation. As time went on, you could talk to him one day and he'd be great, and maybe the next he might be down, feeling the effects of the disease.

The last time I saw V was in his final days when he was at Duke University Hospital with Pam and his mom. He was having a really difficult day, getting sick from the treatments and in such pain on top of that. In fact, by that time, he was so sick and in so much pain that he was set up to where he could administer himself morphine at will, even though he hated to do that because of how it made him so sleepy. But whenever he was awake and alert, all he talked about was the V Foundation and finding a cure for the disease and how our society had just kind of accepted cancer with a certain level of apathy. He talked about what we could do to conquer this disease, and never did he talk about his own misfortune. When I walked out of the hospital that day, I wasn't thinking that that would be the last time I would see him. I walked out motivated by him, motivated by his spirit and drive even when he felt as bad as he did. I almost felt bad about feeling so upbeat, but that's the effect V had on people. He touched people for the better.

⚬⚬⚬⚬⚬

*The day before he was scheduled to go to California to join his good friend **Bob Lloyd** for a golf tournament, Valvano called ahead to say that he had just been diagnosed with cancer. Lloyd remembers when Valvano broke the news to him:*

It was a very difficult thing to hear. But even when this was going on, he had been able to make light of it. The story is that when the doctor showed him the x-rays and pointed out the dark areas indicating where the cancer was, Jim said, "That's because you didn't use the flash attachment. Use the flash attachment!"

What's amazing about Jim was the way that he approached things. He was now in another battle, another fight, and he was going to work very hard at doing everything he could to fight the cancer. In the end when he knew he couldn't win the

No college basketball coach was more animated along the sideline than Valvano, who seemingly looks heavenward for help in the first round of the 1985 NCAAs. His prayer was answered as the Wolfpack held off Nevada-Reno in a first-round game in Albuquerque, New Mexico. Later, when Valvano had cancer, he again looked up for divine inspiration. (AP/Wide World Photos)

battle, that's when he put things in motion to start the foundation. Once again, Jim was the coach and he set out to put his team together. He put the board together with business people and some celebrities. I remember when I went up to visit him while he was at a hotel in Connecticut, and he told me, "Now, I'm going to need some people who can help raise money, and I need some business people to help run the business side of things." We talked about that, and he was the coach.

The hotel in which we had that meeting was the Radisson in Bristol. That's where Jim stayed while up there doing some of his work for ESPN. This brings up an interesting story. Four times a year, we have board meetings for the V Foundation, and we move them around. This year we had a meeting up at ESPN. We would be staying at the Radisson in Bristol, and I didn't think much about it. I just remember that it was the hotel at which Jim and I had stayed up until two o'clock in the morning that time back in 1993 thinking about the creation of the V Foundation. Talk about coming full circle: Here we were eight years later, with a foundation that is raising as much money as it does and with eighty-four cents of every dollar going directly to cancer research and awareness.

Anyway, the thing that turned the V Foundation from a regional organization into one with national notoriety was that 1993 ESPYs speech that Jim gave which was televised by ESPN, and for the telecast they played for background music the song "Wind Beneath My Wings." It is a very emotional song and one that I will always associate with Jim. So fast forward to eight years later as I'm returning to the Radisson for this latest board meeting. Just as I turned into the parking lot of the hotel, the song "Wind Beneath My Wings" came on the radio. I mean, what are the chances of that? All I could think at that moment was, Jim, you're still

coaching the foundation. What makes it even more seren-
dipitous is that the song was featured in the movie *Beaches*
with Bette Midler and Barbara Hershey, in which the characters reverse roles with one of the women having to care
for the more famous one, and that plotline could just as well
describe my life with Jimmy.

The V Foundation is a commitment, and it's a commitment that people aren't going to stop fulfilling. We've been
successful the way we have been because we have a board
that really cares about what we're doing. We laugh because
we say we have board meetings that last about two and a half
hours, and thirty minutes of that is just so everyone has time
to hug everyone else.

That reminds me of a funny story involving Mike
Krzyzewski. Jimmy and I played against Mike when we were
at Rutgers and he was at West Point. He and Jim became
very friendly, especially near the end of Jimmy's illness.
Being a West Point guy, Mike is a pretty taciturn person.
With the V Foundation we are just the opposite: We love to
hug and all that at our meetings. So when Mike came to our
first meeting, he looked around and saw everyone hugging,
and during all this Nick [Valvano] went up to Mike and
gave him a big hug. Segue now to a couple years ago when
Duke was playing in the Maui Classic—and I spend seven
months living in Maui during the winter. I go up to see the
game, and after the game I go down to sit near the locker
room, where I see Mickey [Coach K's wife]. And she said,
"Why don't you go up into the locker room and see Mike?"
So I go up into the locker room and there's Mike talking to
the team. They had just beaten Kentucky, the defending
national champions and still ranked number one. Mike's
telling his team, "Great game, but now you're going to be
asked if we're number one, and what you should tell anyone

who asks you that is, 'If we continue to play well and if we can continue to work hard, we can be the number-one team in the country. But we're not there yet.'" Then he turns away and the team starts to walk out, and that's when Mike sees me. I'm standing there not knowing if this is the right place and time to give Mike a handshake or a hug, and he answers that by coming over to me and giving me a hug. Even in that environment, the V Foundation lives on.

⌒▨▨◯

Nick Valvano, *Jim's older brother, recalls how he first heard that Jim had cancer and how the ensuing months became the basis for what the V Foundation is now all about:*

The good things out of all this is that Jim got to see and hear all the testimonies to him before he passed away, sort of like a guy who gets to hear all the good things said about him at his own funeral. It still makes me feel so good to see someone I loved so much respected by so many other people, and not just because he coached basketball. People like Dick Vitale, Bob Lloyd, and John Saunders.

One thing that sticks out about Jim's last year, when he had the cancer, was how ignorant and ill-prepared we were to deal with cancer in the family. Any time a person gets diagnosed, if you are not prepared or don't have the understanding, the devastation is twice what it would be otherwise. You don't know what to do; you don't know where to go; you don't know who to talk to.

I can still visualize being on a pay phone and being told by my brother that he had cancer. I was playing in a golf outing, and my wife had called the pro shop, and they paged me. I called home and she told me I needed to call

Jim immediately. So I called Jimmy and he's telling me that he has cancer. That will stay with me for the rest of my life. One of the things we're trying to do with the foundation is make people aware of what cancer is all about and that the devastation of the message itself should be enough.

The other thing I remember most about his last year was how resilient he was. He went from the stage of saying, "Why me? Why me? Why not you, Nick, you're older than me, you used to smoke, you went through a dramatic divorce?" to saying, "Damnit, I don't know how long I'm going to live, but I'm going to make something out of this." He started doing this incredible research about cancer, and when I would call him up he'd say, "Guess what I just found out!" and he would give me all these statistics. The adrenaline was flowing and there was no pain when he was telling me stuff like this.

The third thing I'll remember is his telling me, "You know, you need to start paying attention to every day. Stop worrying about all that other stuff, and start paying attention to the stuff that really matters because you never know when the rug is going to be pulled out from under you. And finally, please take care of my family."

∞

As great a bench coach as Valvano was and as funny and entertaining as he could be, the most lasting memory of Valvano was how courageously and boldly he battled cancer, numerous times pulling himself together in public to give inspirational speeches that brought the house down. Such was the case in 1993 for the ESPYs, when Valvano took the podium upon winning the Arthur Ashe Award. **Dick Vitale** *remembers the moment:*

My personal feeling about Jim—and I share this everywhere I speak—as I speak now, sitting in my office looking at a gigantic photo on the wall of Jim looking right at me is that, to me, Jim's legacy is not going to be about winning the national championship. What it's going to be is the inspiration and courage that he demonstrated for so many others to see and emulate during his battle against cancer. I will never forget the moment of walking out and introducing Jim when he was the recipient of the Arthur Ashe Award [in 1993].We had had to carry him, literally, to get him on the stage. I remember thinking that, as I stood to the right of him, that he would be able to say no more than one sentence: you know, "Thank you so much," and then sit down. As it turned out, I stood there in total awe for over thirty minutes as he just absolutely dazzled the crowd in one of the more passionate speeches I've ever heard in my life. To be there and to see that and to see him pour that kind of energy in his last moment onstage was just incredible. It's something I'll always remember. I get goose bumps just thinking about it.

What many people hadn't realized at the time was that the day before I had been on the phone with Pam and Jimmy, who were back home in North Carolina, practically begging and pleading with him to come to the ESPYs. Jimmy had just found out that his cancer had spread all over. It had metastasized, and the bottom line was that it was now really, really terminal. And it was the first time I realized in talking to him that he had resigned himself to the fact that it looked like it was definitely over. It just broke my heart to hear him on the phone basically saying that he couldn't care less anymore. I'm paraphrasing now, but in essence he was saying something to the effect that "I'm not worried about the trophies and awards: All I'm worried about are my girls

LeeAnn, Nicole, and Jamie and my wife, Pam," and he's crying and I'm crying, and it's just emotional.

Finally, Mike Krzyzewski sat with him on a plane and brought him in. I'll never forget Mike basically saying, "How are we going to get him up on the stage?" I mean, he's throwing up and sitting in a wheelchair at the time, and still he's got that energy and the spirit. And the other thing that's really very moving is the fact that Jim shared with a lot of his close friends that he really wanted to beat cancer, saying, "I may not beat it individually, but we can beat it if we all gather as a team and go out and have outings to help raise money." I'm so proud to be co-chairman with John Saunders and Mike Krzyzewski every year for the Jimmy V Golf Classic. Last year [2000] we netted about $1.4 or $1.5 million.

I know Jimmy would be so proud to know that there's now a Jimmy V outpatient hospital over at the Duke Children's Hospital, where children can come in for treatment. His name just keeps going on and on and on, and it's certainly not just about winning a basketball game, but obviously that put him into the spotlight and made him a big-time name.

※

Valvano passed away only ten months after he learned he had cancer, but he packed as much life into those final three hundred days as he could, including going back to work as a network college basketball analyst. **Pam Valvano** *remembers those final ten months of her husband's life as a time filled with tears, trials, and tribulations, and a healthy dose of hope:*

He realized during that time a lot of the things that he had missed in life with his being so busy all the time. You always think it'll happen to the other guy but not me. It was absolutely devastating. He did not like to go to doctors before this happened, so for him to have to do that was very unusual for him and very uncomfortable, even humbling. The whole environment in a hospital or a doctor's office was depressing to him, even if you're just there for a cold or something like that.

He was really brave. We didn't talk about his dying. I think he talked about it with Frank [McCann] and Nick, his brother. But he and I didn't talk about him dying much because that would have been an admission of defeat. Up until the week before he died, we were still trying new things, new treatments in an attempt to help him. The doctors would say, "You know, let's try this." I thought if anybody in life could have a miracle happen, because you hear about miracles, it might be him, and I guess I thought, maybe it would be him.

He was raised Catholic and went to Catholic school, and at the end he went to church regularly. I think he was in a good place with God and that he was okay with that part of it.

Our youngest daughter, LeeAnn, was twelve at the time, almost thirteen, and I don't think she realized the whole impact of what was going on. I just tried to make her life as normal as possible. Nicole had just gotten a new job and I knew it was hard for her to see Jim like that. Jamie took the year off from school to do whatever had to be done. Even though he had been gone a lot over the years, the girls just idolized him; they idolized him every minute that he was around. When they were growing up, he would come home and lie down on the couch, and they would climb all over him. Each one of them dealt with his illness differently.

I'm a pretty well-organized person, and I like my life to be organized, and this was totally unorganized. We just never knew what was going to happen at any time. Looking back, I was surprised at myself because I was able to stay pretty well focused and do what I had to do and take charge. For years Jim had been the one to take care of us, and now all of a sudden it was the other way around. I was driving him, and that's pretty unusual, so our roles changed. But if it hadn't been for our friends coming almost every day, I couldn't have done it. Nick came and visited whenever he could, and Bob Lloyd came when he could, too. Dick Vitale would call a lot and he would say, "Okay, Pam, tell me something good. I don't want to hear any bad news," and I would say, "Okay, I'll try." I tried, but there were times I wasn't able to say that things were really that good.

Sometimes I would be the one who would talk to everybody on those occasions when Jim wasn't up to talking with anyone. We got letters and letters, boxes of letters delivered to the house, and Jamie would answer every single one. Everyone who wrote a letter to us got a letter back, and that's because Jim felt that was important. Jimmy's mom was there to help take care of LeeAnn, and my job was to take care of Jim. When he felt strong enough to go to the games, I would go with Jim and sit with him. Whatever had to be done, we just did it.

ᑎᐧᕮᐧᕮᐧᕽᓐᕽᐧᕽᑎ

Frank McCann, tournament director of the Jimmy V Celebrity Golf Classic, was one of Valvano's closest companions in the final days. McCann often would come over to the house to visit Pam and check up on Jim. He would spend hours there cheering Jim up and keeping him occupied with pastimes, such as chess. McCann:

One of the things we started doing was playing chess. Jim

Yonkers was a third guy who joined us for a while. We started out on a regular chess set, and, as Jim would always do, he wanted to move to the next level. So he bought a Gary Kasparov chess game that had sixty-four playing levels. Jim had a style of play that was one way, I had a different style, and Jim [Yonkers] had a third style, and we would combine our forces trying to beat this thing. We were on level one for the longest time, trying to beat Kasparov. But we just couldn't do it—on level one. Finally, one day, and I'll never forget this, we were in the living room when we beat Kasparov, and it was if we had won the national championship. There we were jumping around the room high-fiving, and finally I said, "You know, we're only at level one. We still have sixty-three levels to go." Jim always used to say, "You know, on level one, it's us playing him, but on level sixty-four, if you ever get there, Gary Kasparov comes to your door, rings the doorbell, makes one move, and then he leaves."

We also used to play chess while Jim was at the hospital getting chemo. It was a good diversion for him, and he needed diversions. That was a good one; painting was another. When Jim got really sick, he wrote down ten things he wanted to do before he died, and one of them was painting. Think about that; that's the kind of person he was, wanting to do something completely different from what he had ever done before. He's got this terrible disease and what does he do, he writes down on these little index cards what he wants to do.

❧

Pam Valvano elaborates on Jim's painting:

Pat, Frank McCann's wife, and I decided we would go out to

the mall and try to find a paint set for Jim. So we went out and got this little paint set and had a little table back home he could use. But Jim couldn't stand anything in a small way. It had to be in a big way. The set we had gotten him wasn't big enough. He wanted the big standup easel, and so we got him one of those. Frank brought one over, and we rearranged his office at home so that this big easel would have a place of its own.

Now the box that the paint set came in had this picture on it of a house bordering a pond with a boat on the water. So he started painting that picture. In the middle of the night sometimes, he would be in so much pain that he would get up and go out and resume painting the boat scene. He named his painting "Brown Boat." After he finished the painting, he announced that we were going to have a cocktail party for the unveiling, and everybody had to wear a black tie and a beret, even if you were just wearing something like a golf shirt or whatever. We had it set up so that everyone could have his or her picture taken with Jim and "Brown Boat."

Frank McCann:

During the unveiling party, he would say, "You've got to interpret the painting in your own way. Is the boat going this way or that way? In which direction are the clouds moving? Is the water cold or warm?" It was a great evening.

Pam:

I collect elephants, so the second painting he was going to do was one that had elephants in it. So Frank goes to the library one day and comes back with a stack of books that have all kinds of photos of elephants in them. So we took all these books to the kitchen table and sat down with Jim, going through book after book looking for a photo that he felt he wanted to paint. Finally, he says, "Look, I'm just going to do a mommy elephant and a baby elephant." And that became the second painting.

McCann:

But the elephant painting never got an interpretation.

⟨≋⟩

In the last weeks of his life, Valvano was swamped with cards and telephone calls from thousands of well-wishers, which included **Rich Petriccione**, *his former student manager from two decades earlier at Iona:*

We stayed pretty much in touch over the years, and I was lucky, as horrible as the circumstances were, to get to see him right near the end. He died, I think, on a Wednesday, and the Thursday before Pat Kennedy [Valvano's assistant and head-coach successor at Iona] and I had met up and gone down there [to Cary, North Carolina] to see him. At that point we really knew that he wasn't going to last much longer, and some really close family people were going in to see him to kind of say good-bye. He had his morphine pump and he was letting me push it. He said, "Push it as much as you want, because I'm dying here."

The guy is going in and out of consciousness, and he just looked terrible, and then he says to me, "Pet, do you know where you're going?" By this time, you're humoring him a little bit, so I said, "Yeah, I know where I'm going." He says, "No, do you *know where* you're going?" I said, "Yes, I think

I do; I think I know where I'm going." He said, "Do you know what Yogi Berra said? If you don't know where you're going and you get lost, you may wind up somewhere else. If you know where you're going, you can get there. But you've got to know where you're going." And I said. "I got you; I hear you." It took a lot of strength for him to come out with that, but that was his message in the final days, particularly, I think, to some younger people and, I'm sure, his children. That was his big thing: *Do you know where you're going?*

He really believed that nothing has ever been accomplished in any walk of life without enthusiasm, without motivation, and without perseverance. That was his whole bottom line. Having that direction; you know where you've been, you know where you are, and you know where you want to go. If you have those three things clearly in your head, it's a lot easier to get to where you want to go. There wasn't a day that went by that that guy's head wasn't swimming in a million directions about where he wanted to go. You know he wanted to eventually coach in the pros, and he wanted to be on TV. Even knowing that coaching in the pros can be a lousy deal and you can't be the man like you are on campus, he said, "But if I could win the NBA championship, I'd be the only guy in the history of basketball to win the NBA title and the NCAA title. That would be great, wouldn't it, Pet? Wouldn't that be great?" And that's the way he thought. Obviously, you've got to have a big ego for that, but you also have to have the confidence. He assumed that he would win the championship if he coached in the NBA, and that's the way he would have gone after it.

I think he'd be very happy to know of all the stuff that goes on in his name and how often his name gets thrown around, and the fact that this book about him is being written. His goal was to become a little bit of a legend. I keep watching A&E every night waiting for them to air his biography. It would be a story that might motivate some people, too. Particularly about the way he died.

❦

Like anyone else who had any level of affection for Valvano, **Jerry Tarkanian** *still fights back tears talking about Valvano in his final days when he was dying from cancer:*

I was coaching in San Antonio [with the Spurs of the NBA] when he called from Vegas and told me that he had cancer and was battling it hard, and he brought me to tears. I've got a friend who owns a restaurant in Vegas, the best restaurant in the country. And I used to take Jimmy there all the time, and he had this guy, a real tough guy, in tears, too. He was such a great human being.

❦

Charles Chandler, *a sportswriter for the* Charlotte Observer, *had one of the last, if not the last, sit-down interview with Valvano before Valvano passed away in April 1993. The setting was an ACC game that Valvano was working as a TV analyst, and Coach V was obviously in a lot of pain:*

I was doing a freelance story, if I remember correctly, for the National Association of Basketball Coaches. It was going to be a feature on him for their Final Four issue, and I was also going to use the interview as the basis for another story I was doing on him for the *Observer*.

I knew Jim, but at that time it was tough to get ahold of him with his being sick, but my doing a story for the NABC was probably the thing that got me in the door. The interview would take place after a game he was working as a TV analyst in Chapel Hill. The first thing I remember was how the people there cheered him, and all this stuff about North Carolina versus North Carolina State was a nonfactor. The fans were just yelling, "Jimmy V! Jimmy V!"

He was walking very, very slowly and yet he had a good spirit about him. After he did the game we went back into a room and Terry Gannon, who had played for him and was now a TV sportscaster, was there, too. Terry and Jim were very close. I remember after we got back into this room, a kid came in and wanted Jim to autograph something. And the kid had just a regular ink pen. Well, Jim couldn't use that pen because his hand had gotten so bad because of the cancer that he couldn't grip a regular pen, so Jim pulled out a Sharpie® or something like it with which he could write real smoothly. He got his special pen out and he signed it and the kid left. What Jim then said to me chills me to this day. After the kid left, he said, "I can't write. I have no feeling in my hands and feet at all. All they do is hurt. I can't button my shirt; I can't tie my shoes; I can't tap-dance on a bar at midnight." That was him telling me something so simple— that he couldn't write—in his own special way. He was such an amazing communicator, and he had such charisma.

Those words just stayed with me. He proceeded to talk about his interactions with other people at the hospital, other cancer patients, and he went into how he would go downstairs into a kind of dark, lonely place, yet a place where people connected with one another because they had this in common. They were all hanging on together. The whole thing was just riveting to sit there and listen to him even in the midst of what he was going through. He had a real determination about not giving up, and he made the plea like he did so many times in the last days of his life that he was passionate about fighting cancer—about not giving up and not quitting. It wasn't long after that he was gone.

The whole interview lasted about fifteen minutes, so it wasn't a lengthy time. He said, "You fight with the mind and the will, and if you give up you've got no shot. I'm not giving up." And that was right around the time of his forty-seventh birthday.

Here's another quote he had: "In some hospitals babies are being born and cigars are being handed out; there are a lot of happy grandparents. That's not where I go. We're down in the basement; there are no cameras, no newspaper articles. Everybody's battling the disease that can take their life. It's a very lonely place. Yet, it's also uplifting that everybody cares so much for everybody else. There's no selfishness down there. I'll be ready for treatment, and a guy will come up to me in a wheelchair, he must weigh about ninety pounds. The guy said he used to weigh about 180 pounds, but he got stomach cancer and he can't eat. He says he read the article about me in *Sports Illustrated* that gave him inspiration. Well, he's given me inspiration. He said he's not going to quit and told me I'd better not. People there bring other people up to me and say, 'Hello, do this and sign that.' Sometimes it is burdensome, sometimes I don't feel that good, but I always feel that's where it's a special role I've been given."

That was neat. He kind of felt like he was in this time and this place for a reason. It's for all the people who are struggling, dying, fighting it, and trying to believe in a miracle.

He always had such a way about him. This was the same guy that you'd seen run all over the floor in 1983 and then get to a place where he went through everything he went through at the school [leading to his buyout in 1990] and then he gets out and this happens to him. I can tell you that it made me think a lot about my life. We're talking about a guy who was so alive—so much vitality. There are people like him that you think nothing like this could ever happen to them. But it did.

Out of all the interviews I've ever done, this ranks right near or at the top in terms of how it affected me. I'd wake up in the morning and sometimes it would hit me like, you know, that could be me. And if it ever turns out to be me, then what business do I need to tend to? It wasn't like it was every waking moment for me, but it would just come up and you can't go anywhere for it. It's absolute truth, and it's staring you right in the face.

⁌

Chris Corchiani remembers the last time he saw Valvano. It was on a golf course in the Triangle area of North Carolina. It was late summer and Corchiani was getting ready to leave town for another season of pro ball. While he wasn't much of a golfer, getting a chance to play eighteen holes with Valvano was too good to pass up:

He was already sick by then and I know he wasn't feeling well, but he loved playing golf and he was out there busting my chops as much as ever. I wasn't much of a golfer at the time, and he just rode me and rode me. Finally he said, "I don't get it. How can you be a basketball player and not have the coordination to play golf?" Yeah, he wasn't feeling well, but he hit some really nice shots that day.

One of the Jim Valvano moments I'll never forget came after I was playing for the Orlando Magic of the NBA. He came to one of my games and came up to me afterward and said, "I just knew you would make it up here someday, I just knew it." It was a simple message and yet so powerful. That was one of the most special moments I ever had with him. Very powerful.

❦

Pam Valvano, *Jim's widow, recounts how Duke coach Mike Krzyzewski became closer friends with Jim in her husband's last year of life and how Coach V's death changed Coach K's outlook on life. To this day, the Krzyzewski and Valvano families remain close:*

Jim and Mike played against each other in college and ever since then our lives have been kind of parallel. Jim and I have three daughters and they have three daughters, and now we both have two grandsons. When Jim was sick in the hospital, Mike would come over and visit with him. There were days that Jim would be in there having a bad day, but as soon as the door opened and Mike appeared, it was like Jim didn't feel bad anymore. All the bad things went away. They would just smile and talk, and maybe it was about a game that Duke had just played or one that was coming up—whatever they wanted to talk about.

I think the other thing that changed their relationship was the *Sports Illustrated* article ["As Time Runs Out," January 11, 1993] that was done on Jim. I was against him consenting to the article because I had felt that our life had already become an open book, and I was like, "Can't you even have this disease be private?" But he said it was something he really wanted to do, and after he did it I came to realize that it was probably one of the best things that he ever did. Because of it, people saw a different side of him that they hadn't seen before because they knew him as such a comedian, such a showman, they thought he was up on stage all the time and that there wasn't a deeply personal side about him. It allowed people to see that there was a real person in there.

Mike's wife, Mickie, had bought the magazine and highlighted parts of the article for Mike to look at when he had time because he was so busy during the season and she was afraid he might not have time to read any of it. Mike read it and for a long time, perhaps even to this day, I don't know, he kept it on his nightstand, and Mickie said he would just take it out and read parts of it. When you're coaching and caught up with everything that goes with that, being in the limelight, you have a tendency to forget things that are really important.

Mike came to realize that over the years he had missed things that his daughters had been involved with, so that with their third daughter, who was playing high school basketball, he would even leave his practices to go to some of her games. He realized that there are certain things that you can't get back. Being a coach, there are so many demands on you, but this whole thing changed his life. I think that Mike realized, number one, if you have your health you have everything, and, number two, you can't forget about things in your life that are really important. He is seeing it now after this third [NCAA] championship—everybody is asking you to do a bunch of things and you have to find a way, somehow, to prioritize things. Do what's really important and do not forget your family.

Their relationship changed a lot. When they were at the ESPY Awards, they talked the whole time. Mike flew up there with us to help get him there. It was rough, especially when we had to walk a long distance. Someone asked us if he wanted a wheelchair, and I said, "No, we don't need one," keeping in mind that he had never been in a wheelchair.

125

He said, "Well, Pam, this is a long distance to walk. Maybe I should use the wheelchair." I remember pushing him up there, and it smacked me in the face right then just how sick he was. I didn't have any idea how he would be able to get up there and give a speech, especially the one he ended up giving. Being with him all day, I couldn't help but wonder if he would even be able to get up there in the first place. Now when you look at the tape of his ESPYs speech, it doesn't look like there is anything wrong with him. He was onstage and at his best. It was one of the best speeches of his life and people talk about it to this day. I was amazed, just absolutely amazed, because it was like he could put everything else behind and just do what he had to do.

⚬⚬⚬

Mike Krzyzewski's remembrance of Valvano's last days:

His last six months of life were incredible. He kept getting on that airplane from North Carolina to Connecticut, to go to ESPN, knowing that he would throw up on the flight and that he'd collapse at the end of the night. But he wanted everyone to attack this disease with passion, to pressure the government to go to war against it. A person dies of cancer every minute in this country, but that's just a statistic, it has no feeling. Jimmy gave it feeling.[1]

⚬⚬⚬

Frank McCann talks about the golf tournament, which has become a major annual event for anyone who knew Valvano and has been in any significant way involved with the V Foundation:

ESPN was just kicking off the V Foundation and had started talking about major fundraisers, and Jim just loved golf. We had put on a little golf tournament by itself, and that tournament in itself is its own story because it's the predecessor to the big tournament. He wanted to run a golf tournament for just his friends. No money involved, just friends. This was long before he was sick, and he decided to call it "the Rossi." He called it the Rossi after ABC golf commentator Bob Rosburg. He was always enthralled by Rosburg because, invariably, someone on the telecast would always ask, "Rossi, what do you think about this?" or "What do you think about that?" and he'd say something like, "Well, I think he can hit a four-iron, cut it around a tree, and put it on the green." And nine times out of ten the golfer would do it. And Jim just loved that.

Once you were invited to the Rossi, you were in for life and could never be kicked out. But once you declined, you could never be in it again. It's the opposite of every golf tournament you've ever known, because the giveaways might be something like a Harris Teeter bag with a bunch of junk in it, and we would invite, say, Bob Rosburg's son and not Rosburg himself, or we might invite some famous guy's chauffeur and not the famous guy himself. Dinner was a black-tie, tuxedo affair at Amedeo's Italian restaurant with red and white tablecloths. It is an excellent family restaurant and a place that Jim loved. Everything about the Rossi reeked unpretentious, and that's the way Jim loved it. Everything was about friends getting together.

When he was sick, we would talk about fundraising and golf tournaments, and he said he wanted to create a major fundraiser for the foundation. He certainly now had the time to do it. We talked about it a lot and the mechanics of the thing and how much money we expected to raise. Everything had to be big, and we knew that this was not going to be a small event. About six months after Jim passed away, I contacted one of Jim's friends in the Raleigh area, Terry Pegram of DBM Graphics, and we started putting the wheels in motion on the golf tournament. From there, we formed a board, and it just took off. Now we have twelve hundred volunteers helping out with this thing, and it's just like family. It's a one-day tournament on Sunday, but it starts with a pairings party on Friday night and an informal celebrity tennis tournament on Saturday followed by a practice round of golf and a Saturday night gala with an auction. Then we have a Sunday breakfast followed by the golf tournament. We've had anywhere from twelve thousand to twenty-five thousand spectators out on Sunday to watch the golf. It's huge! Last year alone we netted $1.85 million and in seven years almost $7 million.

⁂

Nick Valvano talks about how much he misses his little brother:

I miss him making me laugh. He was the funniest guy I've ever met. And I don't mean just telling jokes he had heard somewhere else. He could just take everyday situations and make them the funniest stuff you had ever heard—he did this from the time he was a little kid. I can remember being in the sixth or seventh grade in school, and he was in third, and in those days whenever a teacher had a kid with any sort of talent the teacher would take that kid around the school to other classes and have him perform in front of other kids. One day our teacher told us that they were going to bring this third-grade kid around who did this great impression of

Jimmy Durante, and, lo and behold, in comes my brother wearing this hat and getting ready to do his Jimmy Durante impersonation. I was so embarrassed, like any other older brother would be, thinking, *Why does he have to be such an idiot?* But he was funny.

I miss my best friend. I was supposed to retire, and I'd move down here and we were supposed to do the adult equivalent of being kids again. That's sad, you know. You go and do your life, and then something like this happens where the rug gets pulled out from under you. Jim is probably the only person I've ever met who lived each day to its fullest. That goes back to the insatiable appetite to do everything, to be everywhere, to try everything. People who got to know him and got to see the other side of him can appreciate that all the more. Those who got to interact with him in his last few years, after he got out of coaching, got to see him as one of the guys. Jimmy needed some place to escape to, too, like anyone else.

Jim had to make everything he did a game. Everything. He'd pour a glass of chocolate milk and it would be two inches higher in his glass than in mine, so I'd say, "Why do you have to have two inches more?" and he'd take a sip and say, "Now we have the same." Everything was like that with him. It could be, Let's sit back in our chairs at the table and push the coin across the top, seeing who could be the first one to get a leaner. Or maybe it was picture cards. Who could be the best flippers of cards? Those are traits that carried over to his adult life.

He was a very sensitive guy, too. No one can be a motivator unless he's sensitive. Life with Jim didn't have a slow lane. Few people got to know the person, and that's a shame because he was a talent. He's probably more famous now than when he was alive because of his ESPY speech and the visibility the V Foundation is getting. Some of our biggest supporters now didn't even know him as a basketball coach.

⚭

Pam Valvano discusses what her life has been like since Jim passed away in 1993:

Life for me has been different at times. I had never really lived alone. Jim and I dated for five and a half years from the time we were sixteen to the time when we got married, and he was really the only boyfriend I had ever had.

We were married twenty-five years, and now I had to take over the role of taking care of everybody. Sure, I had taken care of the three girls as a mother and him as a wife, but now here I was being the one responsible for everything. Even though Jim had been gone so much, he really took care of us. Not having him around anymore was hard for me. Luckily, the two older girls were grown by the time he passed away, and they were very helpful.

You know, God works in strange ways. Jim was wanting to have a third child. He would have had six if I wanted to. So he talked me into it. In fact, it was a friend of ours, Joyce Driesell, Lefty's wife, who helped talk me into it. She and her husband had had four or five children. One day Joyce and I were sitting around the pool, and I said, "Joyce, I don't know what to do. Jim really wants another baby, and I don't know if it's because he wants a boy or what it is, but I don't know if I should have another baby." And she said, "I think you should have another baby." So I said, "Okay, I'll try," and within a month I was pregnant. There I was with a seven-year-old and a ten-year-old, and now it's starting all over again. All of a sudden reality hit me, like "Wow, my life is going to change all over again." And then when Jim died, I had this child [LeeAnn] who was almost thirteen years old and who needed her mom. I couldn't give up and say something like, "Okay, I don't want to live anymore." I had a child who needed me, and, boy, did I need her. It was a great feeling to feel needed, and so she and I became best friends.

I'm close to all of my daughters in different ways. Now my [two older] girls are mothers and they look at me differently than they did while growing up. Now they look at where they are and say, "Wow, you did all this for us?" They just thank me all the time. Nicole recently wrote me a card that says, "Thank you for the last thirty-one years," and I could just cry. She said, "All of your hard work over the years has made Jamie and me the mothers that we are today, and we're now reaping the benefits of all your hard work." You can't ask for anything more.

Going back to when LeeAnn was younger, she gave me a reason to go on and to focus on taking care of her. When the time came for her to go away to college, it had been five years since Jim had gone, and I was in better shape [emotionally] then; it was okay for me to be alone for the first time in my life. But the other two girls were here and now our families have grown with grandchildren, so everything keeps changing. It's amazing to think that it's been eight years since Jim died. It does not seem possible. It has all gone by so quickly.

Another thing that is amazing to me is the impact that he made on people. There's not a week goes by that I don't see somebody who tells me how they met him, what they thought of him or the ESPY speech, or you name it. And we're talking eight years later. When they hear my name, they ask, "Are you Jim Valvano's wife?" I say yes, and they go on with their story.

CRULO

Less than a decade into its existence, the V Foundation had raised about $20 million for cancer research, and [foundation board member] **Dick Vitale**'s *only regret is that Valvano isn't still around to see all the success his name has generated:*

He would be so excited to see the growth of the V Foundation. Jimmy would be going nuts knowing this. It's amazing, the research that's being done with his name—places, rooms that have been established at the University of North Carolina and Duke. A lot of it, I believe, was generated by his famous ESPYs speech, the most sensational speech I have ever heard. In fact the next day when I got back, my phone was flooded. My answering machine had calls from coaches all over the country saying they hadn't realized how sick he really was, and, "My God, please, Dickie, please tell him we're thinking about him." It had been less than twenty-four hours from the time that he spoke, which was about eight at night. Well, the next morning I get home and that afternoon I called his house and his wife Pam says, you know, she's like crying and saying he's not coming to the phone for anybody. And I said, "What?" She said the phones have not stopped from people that heard him on the telecast. Johnny Carson and President Clinton were among those who had called. She finally got him on the phone for me, and it was the last time I actually ever heard his voice: It was very low-keyed, like a whisper, like, it's over, we're not going to see him anymore. I told him, "I just want you to know about the coaches who called and said you were unbelievable last night. You have so many friends."

You get a little emotional at times thinking about it. But Jimmy made a great impact on so many lives other than basketball with his speech that he gave on that ESPYs Award show.

౷

Michael Warren explains how Valvano's decision to start the V Foundation was a stroke of genius, not just for how it has raised millions of dollars for cancer research and awareness, but in the sense that it was a way for Coach V to live on in people's lives long after his own death:

Because of the foundation, he'll live forever! Not only will he live forever in the sense that some famous people live on in people's minds, but in the sense that he created and then left behind a legacy that remains such an active part of our lives. There are people supporting or benefiting from the V Foundation who don't even have a clue who Jim Valvano was. He's living now because of the V Foundation, which in turn has left Pam and their daughters with another way they can actively remember Jim. To me, that's huge.

4

THE VALVANO LEGACY

There are many ways to remember Jim Valvano: as basketball coach, as network TV commentator, as radio talk-show host, as family man, as motivational speaker, as golf nut, as English lit fanatic, as crusading cancer patient, as businessman, as friend and confidante, as TV sitcom guest star, as David Letterman guest, on and on. There is no easy way to pigeonhole Valvano, and that's the way it should be.

∾

Nick Valvano, Jimmy's older brother by three and a half years, gives some background on the Valvano family and the role athletics and coaching played in their lives:

We grew up in Queens in an area almost entirely Italian. Children of first-generation Italian Americans. We were very close and age meant very little. When Jim was born, my dad told me, "Now you have another responsibility and a brother to take care of." When Jim got old enough to walk, he went everywhere with me. I don't think Jim had any real friends his own age until we moved out to Long

Island when I was about sixteen, and he was just going into the eighth grade. He had friends when he went to school, but when it came time to play stickball or basketball or football he played with all of us older guys, which is why he got better: He was always competing with older kids.

In the early years of our playing together, my father would say, "Let him get a hit. Let him win." Well, after a couple of years, he was really doing it on his own, winning and so forth, and getting confident and arrogant, and my father would say, "Why are you still allowing him to win?" And I'd say, "Dad, we're not; he's doing it on his own." By doing all this, we became very close. We played all the games at home together, like ping-pong or that board hockey game. So he was my best friend, and I was his best friend. As we got older, even though the gap was the same number of years, that "gap" got a little wider when I got into high school. Once he got into college and I was in graduate school, we were close again.

Jim might have been one of the most competitive people I've ever met. He loved to compete and he loved to win. If he hadn't had that, he never would have been able to play with us older kids when he was nine years old. That's made him what he was. He was about six feet tall and a hundred sixty pounds when he got out of high school, and he was able to get so much out of himself physically because of how strong he was mentally. That desire to compete. And he had no fear, even when he was a little ninety-pound kid all nose.

I often tried to look at Jim as not being my brother, just to try and get a different perspective. When somebody would say to me, "What's the thing you thought about the most when he died?" and I say, "That I lost my brother. Yeah, he might have been a celebrity coach and on Johnny Carson, but I remember him when he slept with a teddy bear." Just now I'm starting to realize what the public had seen in him all these years. When I looked at Jim, I still saw my brother, the same guy who when he was small I would turn to my friends and say, "Watch. I can make Jim cry within five minutes so that he would then go home. Of course my dad will beat me up when I get home, but watch this." That's what I remember.

∽∾

Pam Valvano talks about how she came to know Jim:

I met Jim when I was in the eighth grade. His dad [Rocco] was the basketball coach and athletic director at Seaford High School in Long Island. Jim came into my class and we got to know one another, but just as friends. Then in the ninth grade, the tenth grade, the eleventh grade, I would go out with different boys, but not Jim. He wasn't really dating girls at the time. He was so into sports like baseball, basketball, and football, so he was the consummate jock. I don't think he really cared much about girls then.

The boy that I had ended up dating had graduated the year before and gone off to college. I really wanted to go to the junior prom, and I didn't think my boyfriend would be able to come home for it. So I asked him if he would mind if I went to the prom with someone else, and he said no, as long as I would make it only one date with whomever I ended up going with; no big deal. Jim found out that I was looking for a date, and he asked me to the prom, and it was obvious to me that he was totally inexperienced when it came to dating girls. So we went to the junior prom together, and after that, I don't know what happened, but we just started dating. I broke up with the other boy and dated Jim for five and a half years, including all through college.

When he was at Rutgers, I would either drive there to New Jersey to see him or wait to see him when he came home. And we got married when we were twenty-one. He graduated in May, and in August of 1967 we got married, and right away we started on the roller coaster of what coaching was like. First it was two years with him as an assistant at Rutgers and then it was on to Johns Hopkins in 1969 for one season in his first job as a head coach. That was very unusual because here we were, twenty-three years old, and some of the kids that were playing on the team were twenty-one. So, basically, we were the same age. A lot of the kids came from

Valvano and wife Pam arrive at Los Angeles International Airport in April 1988 for his interview with UCLA officials regarding the Bruins' head-coaching position. Valvano ended up staying at N.C. State, but only for two more seasons before his dismissal. (Mark Gostin photo for AP/Wide World Photos)

pretty well-to-do families and were very smart—with some of them going into pre-med and other professional courses of postgraduate work.

∽∾

Nick Valvano left behind a career in sales and marketing to move to Raleigh and become the executive director of the V Foundation. It is one of his ways of honoring his little brother, who knew he was something special from an early age:

He was such a complex guy because he had this insatiable desire to do everything, to know everything. If he hadn't had to sleep, he wouldn't have slept at night. There was always something else that he wanted to do. For example, he read, a lot, but he [rarely] read fiction. Fiction didn't teach him anything. He would read all these nonfiction books and remember a lot of what was in them.

What impressed me about my brother the most was that he was interested in multiple things. He wasn't only a coach. He was interested in business and interested in people, why people did things, and how you motivate somebody to get the maximum out of them. He was a contradiction. He was arrogant, yet insecure; he was optimistic, yet he was depressed at times. He had this personality that there was no gray. People who are this way have these highs and these lows. They're afraid of failure, but they're not afraid to go after something and try to succeed. What keeps them going is the paranoia of failing. Like Satchel Paige once said, "Don't look back over your shoulder, someone might be gaining on you." That's the kind of attitude Jim had.

As his older brother, I just feel it's a shame that people didn't get a chance to see who he really was. He was just starting to realize that he could really do all the things that he wanted to do. He would watch the *Tonight Show* and say, "Hey, I could do that," and, you know, he probably could. "Standup comedy? I could do that." He'd look at me and say, "Business sales and marketing? I could do that, too," and he'd really mean it. And he probably could have done those things, too, and done them well. The only reason he didn't do those things was because he didn't have time to do them, and he had always been that way as a kid.

At a very young age—and I think you have to be very fortunate to have this ability—he knew what he wanted to do. To be so damn sure that's what you wanted to do, that you could set down goals, and as you got older and more exposed to the things involved in that profession you had identified when you were younger, it would further ingrain in you that that's what you wanted to do. How many people can say that about their lives? Jimmy could. I'm on my third career after starting out as a teacher and basketball coach. Then I became a sales executive and now I'm a fundraiser. I'm not sure what all the attributes to that are, but I guess you have to be someone who knows yourself very well. He never said he wanted to be a fireman. He never wanted to be a policeman, and he never wanted to be a doctor. He always wanted to be a coach.

෨෩෨

Rich Petriccione, *a long-time Iona administrator, admired Valvano's enthusiasm for life and how it rubbed off on almost everyone around him:*

Kids who played for him knew that he was real special. Even on those days when he would go somewhere for a coaches' meeting or whatever, I would miss him. You liked him so much that it was easy to be possessive of him and want some of his time. He was just that kind of guy. When he was gone, it would certainly be quiet. There would be a void, but whenever he showed up, he was a whirlwind. It was almost electric when he entered a room. Like any clown, you can't be "on" all the time. But if you egged him on a little bit, you could get him going. And he did like to perform. He'd get it going for you.

Just recently I met a guy whose name is actually Larry Turtle, and I've seen him a few times since, and it got me to thinking about what Jim's reaction would have been in meeting a guy named Larry Turtle. It would have been vintage V. If Jimmy were here, he would see this guy and just go into an incredible soliloquy, something like this: "Wait a minute. You're name is Turtle? And your mother is Mrs. Turtle, and your father is Mr. Turtle, and you are Mr. and Mrs. Turtle's son? You're part of the Turtle family along with the Hares, right?" Now remember, this would be a guy he'd never met before, and whether he was the president of IBM or a local bus driver, Jim just couldn't help himself with people like that. He'd say, "Oh, my goodness, you ought to meet this guy. This guy is a turtle. You don't look like a turtle, but you're a turtle. I've seen lots of turtles before, but I've never seen one walk so erect for a turtle." Always joking. He wouldn't stop. And so now I'd be laughing and Turtle would be laughing and you would be laughing, and then he'd, literally, with a hand wave, call a few more people around to meet the guy. People would come over and try to see what all the commotion was about. I'm just paraphrasing what he might have said. He knew how to take the ball and run with it.

⚬⚬⚬⚬

Ray Martin spent eight years as an assistant under Valvano at N.C. State, returning to basketball in 1980 after spending three years working on Wall Street following his graduation from Notre Dame, where he had played guard under Digger Phelps. Martin talks about Valvano, the coach and mentor:

He had a lot of faith in me, and I learned a lot from Jimmy. He was someone who epitomized the same values my mom and dad had instilled in me in regard to hard work and being a good citizen. He had a saying that he would say to the coaches as well as to the players, including those he was recruiting at the time: "I can't guarantee that if you work hard you'll be successful, but I can guarantee that if you don't work hard, you will not be successful."

Every Christmas, when we were in town not playing in a tournament somewhere, Jimmy would always have the coaches and some of his best friends come over to his house to celebrate Christmas with his family. That, alone, was a great experience. I remember one time when my oldest daughter Nina, who's now nineteen and was six years old at the time, and Jimmy's youngest daughter, LeeAnn—they came into the living room on Christmas Eve singing Christmas carols. They didn't know the words, but they sure sounded good and we all really enjoyed it. When Christmastime comes around, I still think about Jimmy and the time we spent with his family at that time of year.

༄

*During **Martin**'s eight years as a Wolfpack assistant under Valvano, he soaked up as much of the effervescent coach's style*

and knowledge that he could. He still carries much of that round
with him as the head basketball coach at Long Island University:

I'm the youngest of eight children in my family, and I was
the first to go to a large university and receive a scholarship
and so forth, so you know that my parents and my family had
the biggest impact on me. Jimmy, too, imparted values on
me, such as the importance of having a positive attitude as a
leader. He was someone that I, as a young twenty-five-year-
old coach beginning his career at the highest level in college
basketball in the ACC, could look up to.

I carried home every word that he would say to me. He
brought me along real nicely. He didn't just throw me out to
the wolves. He was very honest in his assessment of my skills,
my ability to work, and my potential to be a head coach. He
was telling me what I needed to do to get to where I wanted
to be. We would have long conversations, you know in his
office, or in his home, down in the basement, while we were
shooting pool. He would always say, "Keep working hard. It's
tough; you may not progress as quickly as you want, though.
Things take time."

I'm forever grateful for having spent eight years with
Jimmy because I got to see a true professional at work. Jimmy
did it all. He was a speaker, a motivator, a fundraiser, and he
won games; he did TV, he did it all, and we're talking about
the early eighties when college basketball coaches weren't
doing all this stuff. Jimmy set a new standard, and now we
have a lot of great coaches who are doing what Jimmy was
doing twenty years ago.

He was always ahead of his time. Just to see the master
at work doing his thing, spreading his joy and enthusiasm
and passion to everybody he touched and talked to was
inspiring to me. He gave me a little insight on how one

should try to operate a program and deal with people. I try to think back to that all the time. I look at tape I have of N.C. State games and interviews with Jimmy. In watching these, I find myself trying to remember how Jimmy would do this or do that, and if he was in this situation, what would he do? What would Jimmy do? How would he handle it?

He had a tremendous impact on my life as a coach and my wanting to become a coach and staying in the profession. He said you must have a love for your team and be able to take care of your ball players in terms of being there for them. In my later years with him, he also instilled in me more and more the importance of family. My oldest daughter and his youngest daughter are about the same age, and back in those days we would sit and talk about raising girls and how it was different from raising boys and so forth; the ups and downs, and trials and tribulations that teenagers would get into that we had to deal with as a parent.

Looking back, we had grown up in the sixties, which gave us a great historical perspective on the important events of our generation, such as the Vietnam War, Woodstock, civil rights, man on the moon. We had great conversations, and he was always the type of guy who could bring all that stuff down into real layman's terms and talk about those things from the bottom of his heart. And he could talk like this to anybody. Jimmy could talk to the janitor at N.C. State as easily as he could talk to presidents of corporations and universities. And he made them all feel welcome. He had that gift.

I miss him a lot.

⌒⌒⌒

Jerry Tarkanian and Valvano coached more than two thousand miles apart from each other, but they became fairly close friends, perhaps because each had a bit of "rebel" in him. The Tark recalls his association with V:

We got to be really close friends because of our mutual association with Nike; he was a Nike coach and I was a Nike coach, and for a six-year period we were their top-dog speakers. We would speak at every clinic together, and we'd always go out together and then during the summers our families would go on vacation together. My family and his family got very, very close.

I've said this before: Jimmy was the smartest, most intelligent basketball coach that I've ever known, and by that I mean he could talk about anything. I remember being in a Jacuzzi with all the coaches on one of those trips and most of the coaches could just talk about basketball. That's all they know. But he'd be talking about the stock market, he'd be talking about politics. I mean, he could talk about anything. He was amazing.

The trick is he hardly slept. He would sleep only four hours a night. And he would read. He told me he read thirty pages every night. He could recite poetry. I don't know exactly what it was . . . but he's got to be one of the smartest coaches ever as far as pure intelligence goes. On our Nike trips we would speak on a Saturday night and would then go out and wouldn't get back in until about two in the morning. I'd then sleep in because I've got to get my rest, but he'd catch the 6:00 A.M. flight to go someplace else. He was always on a 6:00 A.M. or 7:00 A.M. flight. He was amazing.

He was so funny and he was so great and easily the best speaker of any coach that's ever been around. Every summer, Nike would take us coaches on a vacation and we would go to the best places like Maui and Jamaica. He'd take his family and I'd take mine. It was just a fun trip.

❦

Terry Gannon, now a sportscaster for ABC and ESPN, was one of Valvano's first five recruits at N.C. State. Once Valvano visited the Gannon household in Joliet, Illinois, to recruit young Terry, there never was any doubt where the six-foot guard was going to play college basketball. Gannon:

Within five minutes of meeting Coach V for the first time, I knew I was going to N.C. State. It's just because of who he was. Being around Jimmy Valvano was like being at a heavyweight championship fight or being in attendance at Game Seven of the World Series. Even in a crowd of celebrities and comedians the caliber of Bill Cosby, as I found out later, when Coach V walked into a room, people gravitated to him. I can't really explain it. I feel so lucky to have been around him for the part of my life I was, just to experience him. Maybe that's how Pierre Salinger felt when he was hanging around John F. Kennedy.

Anyway, when Coach V came to our house that time recruiting me, it was immediately clear that he was a special kind of person who would make you want to stop whatever you were doing so you could listen to him. Within a few minutes, he had loosened his collar, taken off his tie, and had his feet propped up on our coffee table. He felt right at home with us, and we felt like he was already a part of our family. He stayed a couple of hours and must have spent an hour and forty-five minutes of that time talking to my dad about basketball, because Dad was a basketball coach himself, and Coach V was telling him a whole bunch of stuff about teams that were playing that night.

One regret I have from my time with Coach V is that I

never took a tape recorder into the locker room before one of our games so that I could have tapes of some of his pre-game speeches. Those were special moments; the motivational thoughts he would come up with. If I had recorded those and kept them for posterity, there would never be a need in my life to have to go to a therapist. I would learn more in those ten minutes than I did at any other time, in or out of school. How he came up with the subjects for his talks and then tied them into the games we were about to play was beyond me, but he could really pull it off. I remember one time before we played Virginia in 1984—a game that was key to our making the NCAAs that year—he went on for about twenty-five or thirty minutes, working into his talk our founding fathers and how this great nation got started and making it fit perfectly into our getting ready for the game. Finally, the assistant coaches had to do *The Gong Show* thing and cut him off because we had to go out and play the game. We lost the game, but it was a speech that I've never forgotten—one among many.

◦◦◦◦◦

Jerry Tarkanian pinned Valvano's success as a coach down to his astuteness:

His coaching style was different from most people's. His great strength as a coach was how sharp he was. I mean, he would come up with all kinds of gimmick defenses, and that's where we differed so much in our coaching style. My teams have always been pressure-defense type teams. People always kid me, saying, "Tark, what the hell are you doing out there guarding guys thirty-five or forty feet away from the basket; they can't even shoot way out there?" He downplayed his coaching, but he was tremendous. I just loved listening to him.

ᏱᎻᎪᎾ

Valvano was a master of extemporaneous speech, able to jump from topic to topic in a near-seamless, stream-of-consciousness manner that made Sports Illustrated *reporter* **Alexander Wolff**'*s job all that much more fascinating:*

I don't think he prepared for interviews in the sense of having something in the can even before a reporter asked him anything. There was a real consistency to his personality. He was very open; he would speak his mind. He liked to refer to characters from his past with no more than nicknames. It was his own constructed world, much in the same way Bill Cosby had characters like Fat Albert and all those people. That was part of what Jim did, whether it was referring to his brother, his parents, or friends—these were very sentimental constructs for him, and he kind of took the tack of "Look at me, the schmuck that I am. Here I am in this wonderful place." And he would carry that all the way through to the very end.

In that speech he gave at the ESPYs, he reworked the same theme of examining where you are in life at this very moment and being hard-pressed not to think anything other than, "This is the greatest place you could possibly be." I got that sense about him the very first time I met him.

ᏱᎻᎪᎾ

Valvano was the master of the restaurant dinner shtick, an effervescent comedian who could spout knee-slapping jokes and stories for hours on end, sometimes at the risk of offending nearby patrons, as **Wolff** *recalls:*

In Springfield there was a luncheon at an Italian restaurant, and there were a couple of Catholic priests in the back of the room. Valvano really got carried away giving this monologue, his usual standup. He started to go into some blue material, and that's when he noticed the priests and started to apologize to them. But then, of course, after apologizing to them, he couldn't resist throwing in a few more racy jokes, some of which involved a priest.

One of them got up and walked out. Seeing this, Valvano, who was the type who always wanted to make a friend of anybody in the room, felt he needed to get this guy back on his side and started falling all over himself apologizing but being unable to fully apologize without sort of continuing the whole shtick. It was a little awkward, but it showed that the guy had no pretense to him. He was going to go down that road because that's who he was.

❧

ESPN college basketball analyst **Dick Vitale** *has often been accused of excessive hyperbole in touting the exploits of coaches, but with both feet on the ground he explains how Valvano's winning a national title at North Carolina State really was something worth shouting about:*

Winning a national championship takes a coach to a different level in terms of what his peers think about him, what people in general think about him. It's unfortunate in a way that a lot of great coaches have never won a national championship, even when people on the inside really know how good they are. With all the visibility and exposure involved with the game today, there are so many people out there who are not basketball fans during the course of the year who get involved

149

during the NCAA Tournament, and the resulting visibility and marketability allows an individual to grow professionally.

Jim was a perfect example of that. Anybody that knew Jim knew that his kids played with a lot of inspiration, with a lot of intensity, with a lot of emotion, and they knew that he had great control of what happened on the sideline. He and Al McGuire were two of my favorite people because the bottom line with these guys is that they had great, great ways of orchestrating and really managing a game. I'd take them over all these guys who just roll the balls out, put on a bouquet, and come to the game. Jim and Al had a great feel and knack for personnel. They had a feel and knack for the tempo of a game, and they just had a great understanding of what it took to win and how to get the most out of their people.

Both Al and Jimmy were in situations where they did win the national title. First it was Al walking away in 1977 with a national title for his swan song—just a great emotional moment—and then Jimmy in '83. What made it so special for Jimmy was the drama involved, because here was a team that all year long had struggled just to get an NCAA berth. They had to go out and win the ACC tournament, along the way beating the likes of Virginia and North Carolina. Both were top-five teams; there was [Ralph] Sampson with Virginia, and then Jordan and his gang out of North Carolina. The Pack had to win those games just to get into the tournament, and then they win an overtime game against Pepperdine in the opening round, march on like they did to the Final Four, and then ultimately hooking up with a team that created a matchup that sort of looked like a David-Goliath situation. Houston had its Phi Slamma Jamma with [Clyde] Drexler and [Akeem] Olajuwon, which is why no one gave N.C. State much of a shot, but Jimmy and his kids really got into that game, managing the tempo well and getting the Cougars to the foul line. Jimmy did a brilliant job getting his team to where it could get the game down to the final moments and open the way for them to win the national title. And then, obviously, at the end of the drama I see this guy running around the court looking for someone to hug and just showing and pouring out all his emotion. It was a great moment in college basketball.

⚭

Chris Corchiani, who played four seasons at N.C. State before embarking on a pro career that has taken him all over the world, to destinations such as Spain, Italy, and Turkey—puts Valvano at the top of his list for coaches who were able to push players to test the limits of their ability:

When I got there, everyone I met was always talking about how great a motivator he was and how he was always able to get you to play your best. He always seemed to know the right thing to say, and there were times that I looked forward more to his pregame speech than I did the game itself. You just never knew what to expect, except that it would be something really special and different each time out. He could get us so excited about any opponent.

There was one time near the beginning of the season when we were playing some team that wasn't a top-level team. It was one of those games that would ordinarily be kind of hard to get up for because it was one that we knew we were supposed to win. So this one time he begins his pregame talk by saying, "Anyone, anyplace, anytime, you have to remember that regardless of who we are playing, Reynolds Coliseum is sacred ground for us, and when you step in between those two lines out there, you are on sacred ground." That couldn't help but make us even more aware of and prepared for each game regardless of the opponent.

When most people today think about Coach V, they remember him mostly as the great motivator. But what most people don't realize, and what I came to know later, was how brilliant a man he was in so many areas of life. He could recite poetry, quote Caesar, and discuss the stock market. This intrigued me, and one time when I went to visit him when he was sick I asked him how he was able to know so much about so many different things. He said, "You know, when I was coaching, I was so busy all the time that each year I would pick one topic that I wanted to learn as much as I could about, and I would spend months finding anything I could on the topic, whether it be a newspaper clipping or magazine article—and put it in a shoebox, and then when I got time that year, maybe a week here or there, I would pull out the shoebox and start reading and studying everything I had put into it."

One thing I tell friends and family about Coach V is how talented he was, too. Whatever he did, he would try to be the best he could be at it, and this gets back to how competitive he was. Whether it was shooting pool or throwing darts, he was going to be the best, and he was going to beat you.

⟨⟨⟨⟩⟩⟩

Dereck Whittenburg on the Valvano legacy:

He transcended the game. All these coaches today owe him. The shoe contracts. The speaking engagements. The radio show. All that kind of stuff. He was the guy who really broke the ground on all that stuff, which has become a major source of income for college basketball coaches.

❧

*As much fun as **Bob Lloyd** has recalling his days playing alongside Valvano at Rutgers and admiring Valvano for what he
accomplished as a college basketball coach, he says he is proudest
of how his good friend handled adversity:*

After all the junk that happened at North Carolina State in
the end—and I went through a lot of that with him because
we were on the phone quite a bit during that time—there is
one thing in particular that sticks out in my mind about Jim.
That was the Ryder Truck golf tournament he put on for
friends, and at the end of the one-day tournament we would
sing "Thanks for the Memories." Obviously, that was very
emotional the year before he passed away.

I went down there early and saw some guy I didn't recognize, so I asked Jim who it was and he said, "Oh, that's the
guy who was the chief investigator of the NCAA when they
were investigating me." I said, "What?" And he said, "Hey,
he's a great guy." I talked to the guy some later that weekend
and he said, "Listen, I don't work for the NCAA anymore,
but let me say this, if I had a son who was going to play college basketball, I would want him to play for Jimmy." He
even wrote a letter to Jimmy saying the same thing.

The only thing they ever proved in this whole thing
was that some of Jim's kids sold sneakers, and they sold the
sneakers so they could pay to go home and see their parents
at Thanksgiving. So Jim leaves N.C. State under this big
cloud that turned out to be nothing, and then instead of
sulking about it and wondering what's happened to his life,
Jim goes back out and creates another life for himself in
broadcasting. And that shows you the fiber of the guy.

The NCAA every year picks a silver anniversary team

made up of players who graduated twenty-five years earlier and had done something with their lives, and in 1992 I was fortunate enough to be named to that year's team. They fly you back for a ceremony, so I go there with Kay, and Jim and Pam were there, and this was before he had been diagnosed with cancer. We went to dinner because we hadn't seen them in a while, and I said to him that night, "Jim, I was extremely proud of my roommate for winning the NCAA Tournament, extremely proud of that, but after what happened to you in getting knocked down amid false reports and being forced to leave the job you loved, for you to come back and do what you're doing now with your career, I'm more proud of that than anything." I'm so glad that I was able to say that then, because if I had said it after Jim had been diagnosed, it wouldn't have meant the same thing.

⌀⟋⟍⌀

Alexander Wolff *has covered college basketball for* Sports Illustrated *for about twenty years and he has traveled the world in search of many of stories, yet Jim Valvano remains the object of some of his best memories:*

My most vivid memory is my first extended one-on-one with him in his campus office in Raleigh. This was in the early eighties, before N.C. State won the title. If I remember right, it may have been when I went there to do a scouting report on the Wolfpack for the upcoming season.

He had this way of being interviewed for pieces like this. He wasn't the type of guy who would take a question and just answer it. It would be an occasion for a monologue, almost like a standup. Right off he went into this lengthy, "How I read *Sports Illustrated* every week" speech: "The first thing I do is turn to the thing in the back there—'For the Record'—to find out if I died or got fired. Then I turn to the front and read in the Scoreboard, or whatever you call it, the whole thing about the little fish in Wyoming, about the dam, and that we should be concerned about their becoming extinct and what we should do." Basically he was describing the magazine as it existed in the early 1980s, where we would write these impassioned, environmental pieces, and in the back would be "For the Record," which was kind of the alpha and omega of the magazine.

And thinking back, of course, a year later after he won that title, I couldn't help but remember this guy who looked for himself in the most inconspicuous place in the magazine, the same guy who did the original "I own a college; You own a college" thing. I don't tape when I go in to do interviews, and I've regretted that with him. This was a guy I wished I had had the tape recorder running whenever I spoke with him, because he would gallop off at speed and with that refreshingly innocent mind. You didn't want to miss any of the turnoffs during his discourse—any of those little byways he took before getting back onto the main road.

He had every reason to be a shtickmeister, so to speak, because he had just gotten into the world of ACC coaching and was trying to establish an identity for himself, obviously in the shadow of Dean Smith in Carolina. He was just this guy who was trying to do the best he could. I held onto every word.

∽∾∾

Over the last ten years of his life, as Valvano's star continue to rise, he told many friends of his ambition to give the entertainment business a shot. He had had no stage or theater training, but he did have presence and a great sense of humor. **Dick**

155

Vitale recalls the time that he and Valvano guest-starred on an episode of The Cosby Show:

Bill invited us to come on the show, and we had a great time. It was the hottest show in America, and this was at a time when the Cos—who's still a giant in the business—was what Seinfeld became during his run. It was just incredible when he asked us to be on, and we tried to be real cool. Jimmy got to rehearsals a day before I did, and when I got there he grabs me and says, "Unbelievable!" There we were giving high-fives to each other, ecstatic because we were going to be on *The Cosby Show*, and we were laughing like little kids.

Jimmy then says, "You know, he [Cosby] is going to ask us out to dinner, I think." And I go, "Oh, really?" So sure enough, Bill comes out and says, "How about us going to dinner?" So I looked at him and said, "Hey, Bill, we'll get back to you in a few minutes on that. I want to check my schedule, and I'll get back to you." So he said, "Sure." And as he walks out, Jimmy looks at me like I'm crazy and says, "Go and check your schedule?! What are you talking about? This is *Bill Cosby*, man." I said, "We've got to be cool, man," and so there we go again, giving each other high-fives, actually believing we were going to make the Cos wait, and then we go, "Yeah, Bill, our schedule is cool; we can go to dinner with you." And we went to dinner with Bill Cosby.

⚬⚬⚬

If Vitale and Valvano were in awe about going to dinner with Bill Cosby, they soon got over their star-struck attitudes for an enjoyable night on the town for dinner. **Vitale**:

We ate at an Italian restaurant over in the [Greenwich] Village. It was a beautiful place, just a small little Italian restaurant. And that's when we found out what being a star was really all about because nobody wanted my picture or Jimmy's picture. They all wanted Cosby's. In fact, people were coming over to the table and saying to me, "Hey, can you take a picture of me and Mr. Cosby?" Finally, I say, "Excuse me, my name's Dickie V and I'm on TV, too. And this is Jimmy V. We're both on TV. What about us?"

As the night went on, I just sat there and saw it with my own eyes: Jimmy was so funny. You know, Jimmy missed his calling. He should have had his own sitcom. He was that good, that funny. Jimmy was so funny, in fact, that he had the funniest man in the whole world, a guy with the number-one sitcom in the world, rolling on the floor, rolling and laughing hysterically, and I mean it was just unreal. But Jimmy had that about him. I saw that so many times with him, how he could make people laugh. If I did a game at North Carolina State, we would go out together afterward to an Italian restaurant somewhere in Raleigh, and we'd be in a back room there till one or one-thirty in the morning, and he'd be in there just holding court, and when he held court he would go on and on and on.

⚬∽∽∽∽⚬

Linda Bruno, who worked for Valvano in the Iona athletic department, said Valvano never had much of a problem with delegating responsibility and tasks:

He was very, very good at the administrative end of it—he just didn't want to do it. He would rather be coaching than doing that. So he gave people around him more responsibility, which was terrific. He made you feel good; he made you feel like you're worthwhile.

I'd come in in the morning, and he was always already there at work. He got up with his daughters in the morning, come right in to work, and then he'd just sit there and have coffee with us, and it was just one story after the other. He found humor in everything.

One of the things I remember about him was the last time I saw him, which was about eight months before he passed away. It was in New York City, and I went to see him and Pam and the girls, and they were in an apartment there. Jim had just received a set of future *Seinfeld* episodes that were going to air later that year. Jerry Seinfeld had heard that Jim really liked his humor. And Jim said to me, "You know, I love his humor because he takes this everyday stuff that is absolutely true and makes it funny." Then I realized, that's exactly what Jim was like. I had never really made the connection at all the whole time I was working for him. You know, he would make up stories and he just told you everyday stuff that was absolutely true and you're like, "Yeah, you're right."

It was hard to have a business relationship with Jim. Working with him everyday you couldn't help but get involved with his family, with his girls. They were always around. They were always first in his life, so you really got to know them that way. He always included you in family things and was very big about having you over to his house, and Pam was just terrific about doing all those things. It was never nine to five with him. Whether it was work or whether it was "Let's all get together and do this and do that," he was just very, very outgoing.

I know it sounds like a cliché, but it's almost like he ran the department like he ran his team. When something good happened, it was for all of us, and when something bad happened, we all shared in that, too. So it was really a very, very different concept. I think his leadership skills would be a great thing for everyone to know and use.

⚭

Pam Valvano talks about how the 1983 national title changed everything for her husband and, likewise, the entire Valvano family:

The demands on Jim were very, very great. He ended up trying to do too much, and that goes with having a hard time saying no to things. As for things like the Johnny Carson show and David Letterman, he loved that kind of stuff. That's right up his alley. He loved every minute of being on *The Cosby Show* with Dick Vitale as "the V&V Movers."

I would go to the Final Four with him every year, whether we were playing in it or not. We always had a good time. The Nike trips were great, too. They took us to wonderful places. With Jim being the entertainer he was, everyone looked for him to make everyone have a good time. That's what they expected, and he came through. He delivered the goods. Jim was a very, very funny person; it just came natural. I'd hear him saying the same stories over and over again, and I'd laugh every time.

Being with Jim, it was kind of hard to be your [own] person. That's the way it was for twenty-five years. But for the last eight years, I have been able to be my own person. I'm happy to represent him and the V Foundation. I'm not involved in the day-to-day operation of the V Foundation, although I love helping out. I think about getting a full-time job, or a part-time job, but I have too much volunteer work to do.

Jim was a big people person. He always wanted to be around people. When he was in elementary school, Catholic school, he would go, escorted by a teacher, from class to class and do things in front of the classes that would make the

Valvano reminding his players to use their heads during a December 1989 game, early in his last season at N.C. State. (Mark Lenihan photo for AP/ Wide World Photos)

kids laugh. Even at family parties and get-togethers, he was always doing things to get a laugh out of people. And around his two brothers, Bob and Nick, he would laugh all the time.

ᗡᗡᗡᗡᗡ

Frank McCann remembers Valvano as being a golf nut who enjoyed playing a round of golf with an inner circle of about a dozen or so friends, all of whom had to be on their toes—if not their games—when hitting the links with Valvano:

He was a fifteen-handicapper in golf, but if there was anybody you wanted to have on your team, he was the guy. He was very, very competitive. With his having been an English major, someone who cared about being careful with what you said, if you made a mistake somehow, whether it be spelling or common sense, he would make you pay for it.

One day we were on the first tee and Jim was wearing a green 7-Up hat with a green 7-Up warmup suit and a green 7-Up bag—I think he might even have had 7-Up on his shoes—and he walks onto the first tee, and I looked at him and said, "Ah, 7-Up. Where did you get all that?" And as soon as I had said that, I wanted to take it back because I knew what was coming next. He said, "I got it from Pepsi. Or maybe I got it from Coke, I don't remember. But why would you ask me something like that?" I knew what I meant, and so did he, but that's the way it was with Jim.

One thing about golf: It's supposed to be a very quiet game. Well, Jim was anything but quiet. Noise was part of golf when he was around. He used to say, "If my kids can shoot a free throw in front of fifteen or twenty thousand people screaming, then you should be able to make a five-foot putt with me talking. So don't worry about the golf because

I'm going to keep talking and no one's going to stop me." If you wanted to play golf with him, that's the way it was.

Pam Valvano:

Another golf tournament he started was what he called the Ryder Truck, patterned after the Ryder Cup, because he had something with the Ryder truck company. So he asked the Ryder truck people to send him a real Ryder truck, so they sent him one of these little model-sized Ryder trucks, and he said, "That's too small! It's got to be a big truck!" So he gets a big truck about four feet high and four feet wide and actually had it mounted on a trophy, so they had a golf tournament of the North against the South, so that all the northerners who lived around here would play the southerners.

ᏻᎦ

Frank McCann talks about how Valvano was able to work any kind of crowd, regardless of size:

One-on-one, he was the same speaking with you as he was in front of five thousand people. No difference. One time, Mike Martin and I went to New York with Jim, where he was going to be part of a Nike clinic for high school and college coaches. To give you a perspective of the guy, when we went to the Green Room, a prep room, there were all these nationally known coaches in there, and when he walked in, there was a kind of hush and from that point on he took over the room, spinning yarns and the like. Then we went downstairs and in front of something like five hundred college and high school coaches, Jim went through an Xs and Os lecture of basketball that just blew me away. It's the most incredible thing you've ever seen. He had this amazing aptitude for teaching.

 ⌒⟋⟋⟋⟍⟍⟍⌒

Terry Gannon, a veteran network sportscaster, paints a picture of Valvano that makes his former coach sound like a master communicator, which he was:

V was a guy who seized the moment better than anyone I've ever been around, and he did it all without cue cards or notes. He's a man who lived his life without notes. One time he could be talking in front of five thousand IBM executives and have them crying and cheering in the same sentence, and another time he could be in a restaurant playfully wrestling with one of his assistant coaches without any fear or embarrassment about what anyone else there might think. He could talk to anyone in any setting, and part of it was because he was the most intelligent person I have ever known.

One time I rode with him from Raleigh to Greensboro to take part in the ACC's pre-season media day. The drive was about an hour and forty-five minutes, and for the whole time, as he drove, he talked and I listened as all he talked about was Wall Street and the stock market. It was incredible. He knew so much about so many different things. You could ask him a question about anything, anything, and he would have an intelligent answer for you. You had to have a thick skin with him, though. Acerbic is perhaps the best way to describe him. You had to be on your toes around him, or you would be buried by him. If you said something stupid, he would just hammer you, and this wasn't done out of cruelty. It was because he was so bluntly honest, yet would say it in such a way that you wouldn't harbor resentment.

I miss him so dearly in so many ways, like in my job as a sportscaster for ABC and ESPN. Even today, I would love to be able to get him on the phone and have him critique me in ways that would really help me. He could bring out the best in you. In fact, he talked me into going into sportscasting in the first place. I certainly wouldn't claim to have an ounce of his talent, but I think he saw some of himself in me. He was Italian, I'm Irish; he was from the North and was involved with basketball in the South, and so was I; he had had limited talent as a basketball player [at Rutgers] and he got the most out of it, and I think he saw that in me as well.

I spent a little more than a year as a graduate assistant for him at N.C. State, during which time he put me onto his coach's show doing recurring segments. One was called "State Scholar," in which I would interview a really good N.C. State student with an interesting story; the other segment was "Pack Prof," where I would go out and do the same kind of piece on a school professor. He would also let me do his radio show when he was out of town on other business, which turned out to be more often than not. He not only gave me broadcasting experience and a way to put some food on the table, but he was always giving me moral support. When he gave me advice, it was always specific, and he didn't pull any punches. He would tell me exactly what he thought about my work, which is something most people won't do. Of course, there were times it was stuff I didn't want to hear, but even if he wasn't exactly right, he was telling me stuff that most people probably thought but wouldn't say.

❧

Dick Vitale admired Valvano almost as much for his entertainment skills as he did for his coaching ability:

Jimmy was a beautiful entertainer and performer. He did a great job with the one-liners and all the funny lines, the press conferences. He was the media's dream because of the way he carried himself. And I had the good fortune that night of the 1983 title game to be sitting next to his dad, Rocco, at the press conference. We sat in the back of the press conference room, and when Jimmy walked up to take charge of the press conference, Rocco just looked at me and said, "Man, am I proud. Wow! My boy, Jimmy." And you could just feel how proud his dad was to be involved in his basketball and his life as well. He was just so proud to see his son up there.

ᴄᴍᴍᴏ

In the last year of his life, Valvano continued doing telecasts as a network college basketball analyst, even when he was in great pain. He was always able to put on his best game face when the red light came on. But behind the scenes and away from the court, Valvano's family and close friends could see the suffering, as **Vitale** *did during one weekend while up in Bristol, Connecticut, with Valvano doing a studio TV show on March Madness:*

I don't remember if it was a Sunday or Monday that we were to do the show, but the night before, I go to see Jimmy at his hotel room, where he was watching a TV special on the life of Frank Sinatra. We both were watching the show, and there he was lying in bed. By this time he had cancer and was starting to suffer. There he was lying in bed, and all of a sudden he gets up and starts banging the walls and screaming, and then he goes into the bathroom and takes some Advil. I said, "Jim, what's that pain like?" I'll never forget him saying

165

to me, "Take your worst toothache and run it through your whole body." I said, "Why are you here, then? You should be home." But that's the way he was. When he would come out to do a game or whatever, he would just be so spirited about it, about being there.

I'll never forget another story on how I first learned of another side to him related to his having cancer. It was in 1992 while I was down at the Final Four in Minneapolis. We [ESPN] had our set located in the Hyatt Regency. We would come onto the set, and all the school bands would be there. About thirty seconds before going on the air, we were sitting there at the table getting all organized, when suddenly Jimmy would stand up and say, "Oh, I can't take this pain in my back." And I said, "Oh, come on, Jimmy, forget about the pain. Sit on it. You've got muscle cramps, that's all." And then he'd sit down. Well, it was a couple months later that we all found out that the pain in his back was in fact the cancer, which we hadn't known about. It was a tumor. What made it so interesting, or ironic, was that that same year the Make a Wish Foundation had asked me if I would share some time with a youngster with cancer. And I did. Jimmy and I entertained him, and we just had a great time with this young kid. It turns out that that same boy is now working at ESPN in research.

 ⚬⚭⚬

Network TV basketball analyst **Billy Packer** *saw Valvano as a huge talent who might have spread himself too thin with various ventures and opportunities:*

I think that Jimmy was probably one of the most talented business minds in the game. He also was like Bones [McKinney] in that he was a tremendous game strategist. But what happened to Jimmy was he lost sight of the picture of the coach. Because he was so talented like Bones McKinney, he got himself into too many things and spread himself too thin. But he was a guy of magnificent talent in a lot of areas. Unfortunately, I think he realized too late that he should have focused better on the things at hand.[1]

ᗑᙏᗄᓍ

Pat Kennedy, who was coaching at Florida State at the time of Valvano's death, had years earlier been Valvano's assistant at Iona College. Valvano's first game back as an ESPN basketball analyst after learning he had cancer was an Iowa State-Florida State game, at which he was greeted by Kennedy with the following testament:

Every day with you was an exciting day. Every day you had ten new ideas. Every day you left me with a smile on my face, saying, "Boy, that Valvano's something else." And you left me thinking I could do more with my life than I'd ever thought before. Certain people give life to other people. You did that for me![2]

ᗑᙏᗄᓍ

Duke coach **Mike Krzyzewski***:*

We knew each other since our playing days and our early coaching days, when I was at Army. We weren't close friends then, but we knew each other. I don't know if you can become that close when you're competing against each other. But I always respected him and he always respected me.

167

We came down here at the same time. Our ethnic backgrounds and the roads we traveled were all the same. Our styles were somewhat different, although not as much as some people think. I got to know Jimmy really well while he coached at State and even better when he left and got into broadcasting. I think our relationship grew after that. Then when he was diagnosed with cancer, we had a special relationship.

He was a remarkable guy. When you were with him, you were never bored. . . . You knew what you were getting with Jimmy. He had a lot to give. He gave a lot and had a lot more to give.[3]

⟨⟩

Coach K sheds a bit more light on the aspect of heritage:

He was a northern Italian and very outgoing, and in our area there are some people who did not want to embrace that. I think that with some things he was not given the support he needed. We all at times need somebody to stand up and support us. In that moment when he needed that the most, the right people didn't stand up and do it. That's a shame.[4]

⟨⟩

Charlie Bryant was N.C. State's sports information director for many years:

All this business about exploiting athletes and not caring about athletes, well, absolutely nothing could be further from the truth in talking about Jim Valvano. If there was ever a coach that lived who cared about education, it was Jim Valvano. He would get on the team bus and start telling the players how to structure a sentence. I'm serious. On the way to Chapel Hill, he would be talking about sentence structure and how you could change a sentence. He was an English major, and he enjoyed talking and educating people.

I saw Jim many times from my office window go and pull kids out [of their dorm rooms or wherever they happened to be] and take them to class. You can take them to class, but you can't make them work. He tried the old adage, "You can take a mule to water, but you can't make them drink." What Jim tried to do was make them thirsty so they would want to drink. But it's still up to the individual.[5]

ᏩᎻᏍ

Sidney Lowe was a starting guard alongside Dereck Whittenburg on the 1983 national-championship team:

He [Valvano] was very easy to talk to. As time went on, he proved to be just a treat to play for. He would always let you go out and just play your game. If you showed you could do something, he would just turn you loose and let you do it.[6]

ᏩᎻᏍ

*As **Terry Gannon** remembers it, one of the best parts of N.C. State basketball was what happened after the game, win or lose, back in the coach's office. Gannon got a glimpse of another side of Valvano during his brief stint as a Wolfpack graduate assistant:*

As soon as the buzzer went off at the end of the game, my main job was to run out to get some Church's fried chicken, wine, and beer, and bring it all back to the coach's office for what I call a post-game "meeting." Sometimes some of the opposing team's coaching staff would be there and perhaps one of the network sportscasters such as Al McGuire or Dick Vitale. Everyone would be gathered around, and there'd be Coach V with a cigar in one hand and a glass of wine in the other, holding court until about two or three in the morning. He would be telling jokes and stories, but if someone walked into the room once the festivities started, watch out, because if that person wasn't on his toes and didn't have thick skin, he would be in trouble. It was like being seated near the front at a Don Rickles show.

⊙〰〰⊙

A fan letter to Valvano after completing his first season at N.C. State with a 14–13 record:

Coach V,
You don't seem to get the hang of this thing down here. First, you fly to the wrong state. Okay, we can tolerate that. But then you lose to those blue bellies in Chapel Hill and you come back to Raleigh and lose to them again. That's twice in the same season by a few points. We can't tolerate that. I'm telling you I know where you live, and I'm coming to Raleigh to shoot your dog.[7]

Valvano's P.S. on the letter he wrote back to the angry fan:

I hate to spoil your day, but the Valvano family doesn't even have a dog.[8]

5

In His Own Words

Jim Valvano could coach and he could talk. Oh, boy, could he talk. He didn't even need a microphone to get rolling. Many close to him said he could have been a competent comedian able to elicit more than just polite chuckles and applause. He could deliver the goods extemporaneously better than more experienced comics could handle the standard standup routine of canned jokes and stories—although he had plenty of those, too.

Whether it was one on one, one on five, or one on five thousand, Valvano loved having an audience, and more often than not his audiences got a kick out of listening to Coach V. He was incredibly funny, brutally honest, and in touch with his emotions. He was opinionated about many subjects, and he could move people, if not mountains, with his words. He was a terrific motivator, and his words carried a lot of impact, even if at times they went a bit too far. Thin-skin folks needn't have even bothered.

Following is a selection of the best and brightest from the V-Speak archives.

Valvano's practices typically weren't long or repetitious, but they were intense and never dull. (Mark Lenihan photo for AP/Wide World Photos)

On his having an innate sense of humor:

Irony. Absurdity. The irrationality of life. I've carried certain notions—call it an attitude—about our daily existence since at least the third grade. Catching the humor, appreciating the funny side, smiling, laughing, staying upbeat, thinking positive, cracking a joke. These have been practically like commandments in my life. Or maybe crutches. [1]

∽〰〰∾

On giving something back:

I was brought up in a house with tremendous love and concern for each other, with great support and confidence you could become all you wanted to be. And if you made it, I was taught you should give something back to the society that permitted you to have that success. [2]

∽〰〰∾

On life beyond the basketball court:

I want our young people to think that while they're playing the game—the forty minutes on the floor—that basketball is important. But it should be just a part of their lives when the game is over. They should realize the relative unimportance of those forty minutes in contrast to what they are going to do, and attempt to do, for the rest of their lives. [3]

∽〰〰∾

On the player-coach relationship:

The key to a player-coach relationship is communication. It's vitally important that we speak—and speak often— about our goals and dreams. We'll talk about how we're going to obtain them, what obstacles we'll have in our way, and how we're going to do this together. [4]

❧

On preparing for the future, spoken at Iona:

We're preparing our players for the day when the cheering ends. Our players need challenges both in academics and in sports, and that's what we're giving them. Athletes have to be ready for the emotional adjustment of entering the job market. We want our players ready. I'm concerned with people as personalities. Our people want to be cared for. It's a lesson we learned from all the protests of the 1960s. The glamour and lights of the big time are phony. Our kids see through it. [5]

❧

On how he wanted his Iona players to regard him:

I pride myself on being honest with these kids. I tell them they're here first and foremost to get an education. I'm a teacher first and an Xs and Os guy second. I tell them what to expect in the four years here. I want them to know me as a family man as well as a coach on the sideline in a three-piece suit. I want them to see me pulling weeds out of the garden and taking out the garbage.

Playing basketball isn't everything. When they're not practicing or in a game, I want them to enjoy their classes, the campus, and the big city just half an hour away. They have the Broadway shows, the museums, the Yankees and the World Series, the concerts, Madison Square Garden with the Rangers and the Knicks, the pro football teams, and the fine restaurants and the disco palaces. [6]

ᢙᨫᨩᡉ

On his talking so fast:

Everybody said the Valvano family talked too fast, but in that house the subway came by every three minutes and it didn't wait for a lull in the conversation. The view from the top floor: You look out and the subway train is right there. You could almost take tolls. Whenever it rolled up, you had to talk loud. Or with your hands. And when it took off again, speed was of the essence: You had to talk fast because that sucker was coming around again. [7]

ᢙᨫᨩᡉ

On carving out a niche in life:

Initially, there was nothing unique about me or my abilities that distinguished me from the crowd [while playing at Rutgers]. I wasn't quicker than a lot of guys. I certainly wasn't going to be a better shooter or scorer than Bob Lloyd. "What does this team need? Where is the lack? What can I do to fit in?" These were the key questions. Even back then, I think I figured out the answers from a coach's point of view. I could play defense, take the charge, dive for loose balls. Put me on a guy and I picked him up full court, breathed all over him, pulled the hairs on his legs. I was an irritant, a maniac. I did all the blue-collar stuff, but I didn't get the nickname "Sparky" from singing in the Rutgers chorus. [8]

~∞~

On the officiating in the South, spoken when he was still in New York coaching at Iona:

When we lose it's usually because the other team played better, but sometimes the officiating on the road can hurt you. We've played some games in the South where you just feel you're not going to get the best of it.

I've had this happen to me already. I'll meet with the home team coach and the referee before the game and hear the ref say, "Nice to meet you, *Jeeeuum*. It is *Jeeeuum*, isn't it, Mister *Valvayno*? Hope we have a nice game." Then he'll turn to the other coach and say, "Hi, T. J. How's Mary Lou and the boys? Jeffrey still have his toothache? Went hunting with your brother-in-law Alfred. Helluva guy and we had a great time. Let's show the folks a good game." Somehow you just know that you're not going to get the close calls. [9]

~∞~

When North Carolina State offered him their coaching job, Valvano was as enthusiastic as he was clueless. Everything happened so fast. In interviewing for the job, he had said simply he wanted the opportunity and wasn't concerned about salary or length of contract. When he got the call one night from N.C. State athletic director Willis Casey offering the job and giving Valvano only a couple hours to think about it, Valvano spoke to *his wife Pam to get her thoughts. According to Coach V, this is what **Pam** then said:*

"Great. As I understand this, you want to leave a place [Iona] where everybody loves you, you and the president are very close, you've had a great team, financially we're well off, you've got the long-term contract . . . and you want to move where you don't know how much money you'll be making, or how long you'll be making it? Sounds like sound business sense to me." [10]

ᐱᔪᐱᖑ

On his going to North Carolina State and being a second-banana coach in a conference where North Carolina's Dean Smith was king:

The second-class citizen status in the state of North Carolina wasn't about to bother me. I had read where people like Norm Sloan at State and Bill Foster at Duke had been frustrated with all the attention and notoriety accorded Dean Smith and the Heels, that they had been "driven out" of the ACC by it. Hey, I had played and coached at Rutgers, with Princeton right up the road. I had coached at Iona, with Saint John's right down the parkway. Second citizen? I was the second son, wearing hand-me-downs all my life. I was even my wife's second choice. This second-place stuff would be nice and easy for me. [11]

ᐱᔪᐱᖑ

On the rivalry between N.C. State and North Carolina, and him and North Carolina's Dean Smith:

Since Carolina and State had won the last two NCAAs [as of 1983], there were a large number of articles written comparing the two styles of the two programs, the monies spent, the philosophies, etc. I remember one story comparing the Tar Heels' caste system, where the freshmen carried the bags and balls and the tape machine on trips, to our more loose program. Eventually, all the stories got down to comparing the two coaches. Then that led to gossip, at times true but mostly untrue, escaping from behind closed doors. And that led to Dean and myself having our differences as to what we supposedly said and felt about each other. [12]

⚬⚬⚬

On moving up to the "big time" by taking over the North Carolina State program in 1980:

I think I'm ready to coach at the highest level of college basketball. I'm excited and enthusiastic. When I went to Iona, they hadn't had a good team since the French-Indian War. My first job was at Johns Hopkins, and my starting lineup there had an ophthalmologist and a gynecologist. I've really worked up to this. [13]

⚬⚬⚬

On his being recognized a lot in Raleigh:

I'm happy in Raleigh, though I miss the anonymity of going

to a show in New York, where half the audience is more famous than you are. [14]

❧

On preparing to take his first N.C. State team back to New York to play his old school, Iona, in December 1980:

I view it as an "I can't lose" situation. If Iona beats us, it's a testimony to the strong program that I had a part in building over the last five years. If we win, then I'm just going to feel it's a great win for N.C. State basketball, and I'll be happy to be in the finals [of the ECAC Holiday Festival, at Madison Square Garden]. I just can't lose.

Pat Kennedy [Valvano's successor at Iona] told the Iona fans after my last appearance in the Garden that Jim Valvano left to the cheers of nearly nineteen thousand people, and he hoped that people would react in the same way when I return. It's a nice sentiment, Pat, but I'm not sure it's going to happen that way. [15]

[*Valvano got booed at the 1980 game, won by N.C. State, 61–58*]

❧

On becoming an ACC coach when he took over the N.C. State program starting with the 1980–81 season:

There's a certain expectation in the ACC, no question about it. And there's pressure. The first night I was there was "meet the coaches night," and there were fifteen hundred people dressed in red. They don't root for teams; they love them. They don't have any Knicks or Nets or Jets—all they have is their colleges. The schools fill an athletic void. You become a part of their family. [16]

179

◦⟐⟐⟐◦

More on the rigors of coaching in the ACC:

This [the ACC] is really a tough league. Would you believe that when I got to North Carolina State last year I had blond hair, blue eyes, and a little pug nose? And one of the toughest things has been the banquets. I had never eaten barbecue until I came to North Carolina. Well, I've been here 450 days now, and on 317 of those days I've eaten barbecue. Ask me for a dirty four-letter word and I'll say *pork*. [17]

◦⟐⟐⟐◦

On the appeal of ACC basketball:

I love what I'm doing and where I'm at. The ACC is the best basketball league in the country, not because the players are physically better, but because we don't have any professional teams to compete with. People in the ACC are proud to stand up and wear their colors; they aren't waving point spreads. Heck, I just found out last week that we're having a baseball strike. [18]

◦⟐⟐⟐◦

On his first impressions of the South:

They have certain preconceived ideas about New Yorkers, just as we have about them. But we're still both learning about each other. They have their ideas about us, but they're also curious to find out what this *paisan* is all about. I have a certain sense of humor, but one thing you can't do down

there is humor that implies you're better than they are. . . .
I tell jokes like "I can't fly-fish. It's tough casting into a fire
hydrant." When they realize you've come down there with
that kind of attitude, they're more likely to accept you. [19]

❧

On having it good in the ACC:

Here in the ACC I've got the best of both worlds—the fast
lane of first-class college sports and the slow lane of good
North Carolina folks. [20]

❧

On the importance of basketball in Raleigh, North Carolina:

I made a ridiculous statement when I went to North Carolina
State that basketball isn't a life or death thing, but I found
out different. It's worse. [21]

❧

*On the North Carolina State program, not long after he took it
over:*

All this past week I've been saying "North Carolina State,
North Carolina State" to myself. And I liked the way it
rolled off my lips. I liked the image, the great tradition, the
program at North Carolina State, and I figured I was ready
for just that kind of challenge. There just no way I
thought I couldn't get it done. [22]

❦

On his decision to leave Iona and take the N.C. State job:

Hey, we won thirty-one consecutive conference games at Iona . . . and we had a great team coming back next year. But part of the challenge was gone. I had been trying to prepare myself, to gain more confidence in myself as a coach. I thought I was ready, and when North Carolina State came calling, I said to myself that I wasn't going to blow it. [23]

❦

On criticism leveled at him after he left Iona to go to N.C. State amid rumors that the star player he left behind, Jeff Ruland, had a year earlier violated his amateur status by reportedly accepting a $2,500 payment from a sports agent:

I just got off the phone with my wife. She was crying her eyes out. Here she is eight months pregnant, alone in New York. All the reporters are calling her, asking her things, accusing me of this and that.

The truth is that I did not play the [1979–80] season [at Iona] with a player that I knew was ineligible. If I had been aware of it, I wouldn't have permitted it. It's just that simple. The thing that really hurts is just because I'm close to my players, they're questioning my integrity—saying I had to know about it all along. But the truth is that I never heard of Paul Corvino [the agent in question] until the season was over. [24]

❦

On his admission that he had lost touch with star player Jeff Ruland during the latter part of his coaching tenure at Iona:

I'd always thought I had strong relationships with my kids, so the question I was asking myself for several weeks was, *If I'm close, how the hell did I not know about Jeff?* Suddenly, I realized I hadn't been that close for a year and a half. We'd become a good team, and people were seeking me out, and the time I spent with the kids was less. I hadn't had any over for dinner. I had lost touch. [25]

❧

On life at N.C. State in the shadow of legendary North Carolina coach Dean Smith:

I know a fellow named Smith is over at Chapel Hill, and I have great respect for him. But I don't intend to live in anyone's shadow. I'm not worried about it. [26]

❧

On having a center at N.C. State who was one of the tallest players in the nation, although not necessarily the biggest:

Someone told me when I took the job I didn't need to worry, that I had a seven-foot-five center in Chuck Nevitt. I saw him walking down the hallway one day, and he was big. But he turned sideways and disappeared. [27]

❧

On marrying Pam Levine, his high school sweetheart:

With my big nose, she thought I was Jewish, and I thought her name ended in "i." It was three years after the wedding that we realized we had a mixed marriage.

⌒∞∞⌒

On one of his ideas to capitalize on the popularity of ACC basketball:

My fantasy island is a three-on-three tournament for ACC coaches. I'm serious. I'd love that. I can see myself now, taking Dean Smith to the hoop. I figure Virginia would really be tough, but so would we. We'd kick Carolina. With the three-man team, they wouldn't be able to go to the Four Corners. Yeah, we could hold the tournament in the Greensboro Coliseum, and half the money would go to charity and the other half to me. Hey, it was my idea, and the other coaches don't need it anyway. I'm the ethnic kid. [28]

⌒∞∞⌒

On rival North Carolina's knack for recruiting great players:

I'm not going to say that they're lucky, but Dean Smith just recruited his former college roommate's son—John Brownlee, who's six-foot-ten and 240 pounds. I called my old college roommate and his son is in hairdresser school. [29]

⌒∞∞⌒

*On the difference between optimism and pessimism, telling the
story of two brothers at Christmastime:*

The first boy unwrapped a beautiful, shiny electric car. But
he didn't seem happy, and the father asked him what was
the matter. "Well," he said, "I'm afraid the battery might
run down, and the car won't run and you'd be mad at me."
The second boy opened his package and found a pile of
manure. He acted real excited and started throwing it in all
directions. The father told him there'd been a mistake, but
wondered why he was so pleased. "There must be a pony in
there someplace," the boy said. [30]

෧ᚑᚑᚑᚑᚑ

*On the demise of the traditional Big Four tournament,
which had been a popular event featuring N.C. State, North
Carolina, Duke, and Wake Forest:*

That [the Big Four tournament] is one of the reasons I came to
the ACC to coach. You start right off against the best instead
of playing East Cupcake as Al McGuire likes to say. You go
right into the pits. It was one of the greatest things I ever saw:
Sixteen thousand people in that big arena in December.

Back where I come from, people are still thinking about
football, the Super Bowl, and wondering if the [New York]
Giants will win a game. Here we are starting in the Big Four.
What an atmosphere! I lost the first game by four touchdowns—four touchdowns—and I still loved it. I was very sad
to see it go. It was part of the ACC, a fan's tournament. They
took something away that made the ACC what it is today. [31]

෧ᚑᚑᚑᚑᚑ

On losing "the big game":

You can get an awful lot from being a college basketball player as long as you don't get into that "bag" that some coaches want you to get in—that if you lose the big game, that's it. I don't dwell too much on the negative. When it's over, it's over.[32]

❦

On his feelings after winning a game:

To a coach, winning is not so much exultation as it is relief. You're happy if you win a particular game or even a conference championship, but most of all you're relieved. The only ultimate exultation is winning that last game, that national championship.[33]

❦

On obnoxious fans:

There's nothing that is more hurting than having all your friends [and] your family behind you in the stands during a game, and some man starts yelling obscenities and calling you names. It hurts bad. And don't ever listen to a coach who says he can't hear it: He's lying.[34]

❦

On the ACC sometimes using game officials from other conferences, such as officials from the Southwest Conference:

They come in cowboy hats and boots and park their horses outside. One guy called me "pardner" once. The Southwest Conference used to have seven people at their games and here, the places are packed and these guys get all excited. I want our own guys. [35]

ᏆᎦᎦᎦᎦᎦ

On dress codes:

A lot of people think if a kid's in a shirt and tie, he's automatically an altar boy. I'm not into all that stuff. I'm into what they really are. [36]

ᏆᎦᎦᎦᎦᎦ

On the occasional perils of getting out to meet Wolfpack fans, such as at golf tournaments:

I'm the only known casualty of a sand trap. I had a fried-egg lie in a bunker during a round at Myrtle Beach a couple of weeks ago and darn near broke my wrist trying to get it out. Believe me, it isn't easy to go through Wolfpack Country without shaking hands. [37]

ᏆᎦᎦᎦᎦᎦ

On the public speaking aspect of his life as a coach:

It's unbelievable. I do a lot of other speaking, too, and it's gotten to the point that when I open the refrigerator door and the light comes on, I want to give a two-minute talk. When I see three people gathered, I want to go into a speech. [38]

On reading about Vince Lombardi, spoken when he was freshman coach at Rutgers in the late sixties:

I'd been reading some stuff on Vince Lombardi and found a quote I liked. He told his players he wanted the most important things to them to be their family, their religion, and the Green Bay Packers. I figured I could use that, substituting Rutgers for the Packers. So these ten or eleven kids are listening, and I'm giving them this pep talk. Finally, I come to the finish. "I want the most important things in your lives to be your family, your religion, and the Green Bay Packers." [39]

On his perspective when it comes to basketball:

Basketball is not my job as some people think. It's my life. I could no more give up coaching than cut off this big nose of mine. It's part of who I am. I need October 15 [when college basketball practice officially starts] to come every year. It is my biggest and purest enjoyment in life. [40]

On his longtime dream of winning a national championship in basketball:

Back in high school I got hooked on that dream. We won

one quicker [at N.C. State] than I expected. Afterwards I told myself you've got one, now let's get another. You wouldn't believe the number of people telling me I should quit and take one of the TV offers I had at the time. They said I was only going to tarnish it, that the way it happened was so special that I could never live up to that again. They said my whole career had been a Cinderella story and that it was time to get out. They had me all screwed up for awhile. [41]

∞∞∞

On a mid-game encounter with a referee:

I ran down the sideline screaming, and the ref said, "If you say something bad, I'm going to call a technical." I say to him, "Is it all right if I just think something bad?" The ref says, "Sure." So I say, "I think you stink." [42]

∞∞∞

On discipline:

I'm a disciplinarian in the same sense that my dad disciplined his children. He told me he would never do anything to embarrass the family and expected them to do the same thing. That's what I tell the kids. [43]

∞∞∞

On negative recruiting:

It's a nasty business at times. There's such distrust, so much negative recruiting. Every time you say something, it's as if someone's looking for some kind of ulterior motive. [44]

On recruiting in general:

Recruiting is easy. You say to a kid, "What do you want to do?" The kid says, "I like chemistry." You go, "Chemistry, chemistry! We've got the greatest chemistry department in the world! I go fishing with a chemistry professor every weekend!" [45]

More on recruiting:

You have to stay in touch with the kids. And there are so many rules and regulations about when you can call and how many times you can see a player, it's difficult to keep them all straight. But still, you've got to stay in touch. . . . So at least once a week, generally after my Monday night radio show, I'd meet my assistant coaches to make calls. We'd take my office, the secretary's office, and then the other two assistant coaches' offices; we'd have four or five phones going at once. I'd be in there and one assistant coach would say, "Line One, Coach," and he'd tell me where the kid was from, and then he'd stick a note in front of my face with the youngster's mother's name, father's name, the dog's name, the girlfriend's name—not that I don't know them, but when you're dealing with so many kids, to remember it all off the top of your head becomes difficult. So I'd take it and then I'd say, "I saw this kid at the Nike camp, didn't I?" Or, "I saw this kid at Garf's camp. Yeah, I remember now. Sure. I saw him play." [46]

⟨∽∞∽⟩

On whether or not to pay college basketball players a stipend in addition to their scholarships, in light of financial windfalls for schools and coaches from sources such as TV money and shoe deals:

Every player knows how much money is coming into a university and how much the coaches are making; it's not hard to see why some players would resent it. And so I've come to believe that there should be some type of stipend for a player. The problem with this is that if you do it for men's basketball, you need to do it for the other teams as well: women's basketball, the track team, tennis. This is a real problem, but my position would be that a school must bite the bullet and pay the stipend to all the scholarship athletes. What's fair is fair. [47]

ᘒᘓᘔ

On graduation rates of players:

I've always been concerned with graduation rates. Part of the reason I was hired [at N.C. State] was my academic stance. Nobody's pointing any fingers, and we won't rearrange things overnight. But I've discussed this with the chancellor and the athletic director. We're not going to admit kids who don't have a chance to graduate, and we'll smack the ones we take pretty hard if they lag behind academically. I think that's the most important aspect of a coaching job. [48]

ᘒᘓᘔ

On the public's misconception of coaches:

Basketball coaches have become so one-dimensional in the public eye. More goes through our heads than just Xs and Os. Like right now, I want to go and look through that art history book over there. [49]

191

On coaches being categorized:

One of the major failings of the coaching profession is that we've let ourselves be categorized too easily. As control freaks, jock manipulators, X and O geniuses, slick recruiters, game coaches, practice planners. We're either this or that, but we can't be those. Because I was the athletic director and on TV and on radio and did commercials and made speeches and goshknowswhatelse, all I ever got in media Q and A was: "Why do you do all these things?" [50]

On his reputation as a seat-of-his-pants coach:

I know everybody used to say about me that I was a better game coach than I was in practice preparation; a seat-of-the-pants guy who had no strategic plan. Well, coaching freshman basketball made me a game coach. You had no tapes, no film. You may never have seen the opposing team play or any of its players. You may not know their names! Much of your own team may have been unrecruited. So you matched and melded your personnel. Then when you get to game time, you played the first half and assimilated everything you could. At halftime, you made corrections. You whipped serious butt, if needed. In the second half, with all that behind you, you could try to win the game. [51]

On how winning isn't the only thing:

I think I've done a credible job so far, but I don't do cartwheels. I don't judge myself on such a superficial level as wins against losses. It goes without saying that I want to win. That's obvious. But there are other things just as important. I want our players to be students first and athletes second. I want the student body to like our program. I want the support of the alumni. [52]

∽≈∾

On the tug of war that goes on in the coaching world:

There is a real world and an ideal world. And coaches are asked to live in both. You are constantly in that tug of war. Unless you get enough of the Ws, you're out. Well, I may not win all the time, but I'm going to do some nice things before I'm fired. [53]

∽≈∾

On coaches being in line for other jobs:

In my five years at Iona I had interviewed for several other coaching jobs and always felt it to be a positive experience. I used to tell my assistant coaches that if they had the opportunity to find out about other programs in an interview, to jump at it. . . . There's also the fear a lot of coaches have of going for a job and not getting it, and in the coaching business, interviews inevitably result in a strange little mating dance in the media. No school ever wants to admit it offered a guy its coaching job and he turned it down. No coach wants to admit he wanted a job but didn't get the offer. [54]

After a late-season loss to ACC foe Wake Forest left the Wolfpack 21–8:

The Valvano rule of depression: You are allowed twenty-four hours of self-pity after a tough loss. You can curse the gods, ask "Why me?" and think about the what-ifs and buts. Once that's done, you wake up the next day and life goes on. Your little girls say, "Da-da," and your friends call from all over the country to congratulate you on a great season. You've got to go on. That's the great paradox of sports. There seems to be a great importance about a game while you're playing it. Then there is relative unimportance in the overall scheme of your life after it's over. As time goes on, the paradox becomes even more obvious. [55]

⌘

On what he said to then-Indiana basketball coach Bobby Knight after Knight, quoted in a 1990 newspaper article, had said that Valvano's biggest moment in his career—the 1983 national title—had been the beginning of his downfall:

Since you apparently care how I feel, I want to tell you how much it hurts me that you would say those things to anybody, because I have great respect for you and your accomplishments. What you don't know about me is that I love this game. I grew up with the game. My father grew up in it and taught me in it. Winning the national championship was not the worst thing that happened to me. It was by far the greatest thing, and I cherish it above everything else I've done in the game. Bob, I think I love basketball no less than you do. I respect it no less. I have given it no less. I have never done anything to undermine that respect or love. I want you to know that. I care deeply about the game and the coaches and the players, and I want you also to know that my father coached for thirty years and our entire family loved basketball. [56]

༄

On doing media interviews:

The great thing about an interview is that it's a catharsis. It's a very self-analytical situation. Because of all the good, tough questions that I'm asked—and the more times the questions are asked the more times I'm forced to think about my answers. I get to know how I really feel about things. One of the good questions I've been asked is "Where do I go from here?" "You've reached the goal—now what do you do?" Obviously, if we use winning the [1983] championship as the standard, then everyone is a failure in my business. Because there have only been around twenty-five coaches to win the championship in the history of the game. That would make a whole lot of very good coaches failures. Winning the championship would be the wrong standard to use. Let's say that a coach winning the national championship is more like an actor winning the Oscar. You don't stop acting after winning the Oscar. I won't stop coaching after winning the championship. I had the great script and a great cast of characters, and for that I will always be grateful. I'll never forget it, and I'll never come down from it. [57]

༄

On the slow pace of college basketball games prior to the institution of the shot clock:

Basketball is a dynamic game. It's a game of beauty and motion. If I wasn't coaching, I'd be watching basketball. But what we're doing now takes away the essential beauty of the game. It's like a soap opera. You can not watch a program for a week or two, and when you come back you haven't missed anything. You can leave a basketball game with eighteen minutes left, come back with eight minutes left, and you haven't missed anything. [58]

More on the game's slow pace at that time [early eighties]:

Look at the scores of games today. Games in the thirties, forties, fifties. Is that fun for the players? Mine tell me no. Is it fun for the coaches? No, absolutely not. Every possession is life and death. Is it fun for the fans or the media? I seriously doubt it. Okay, then why are the games being played this way? The answer is easy. The guys who control the way the games are played are the coaches and, because of the way the game has become, the coaches have too much to lose. [59]

On his five-point plan to improve the game of college basketball, presented to a Durham Sports Club luncheon in 1981:

One; we can't find three guys who do the job officiating, so I want to use two officials. We lost to Virginia, at our place, on a public mugging. The third guy feels he's got to blow his whistle—out of position.

Two; I'm in favor of a thirty-second [shot] clock. Five years from now we're going to see 8-7 games. The scores keep getting lower and lower. We're also in the entertainment business. You play to win—I vote for the clock. . . .

Three; I don't think anybody should foul out of a game. After the fifth foul there should be a technical, two shots and possession awarded the other team. Also, an offensive foul should be a team foul, not a personal foul. . . .

Four; I want a three-point field goal. It would add excitement to the game and would put the game back into the hands of the players. . . .

Five; All Italian coaches—or coaches with ethnic names—should get lifetime contracts. [60]

ᏨᎿᎯᏓᎾ

On having basketball players who can talk about things other than basketball:

I want the best of all possible worlds. I want kids to be students. I want them to talk about things besides the back door. On the planes I want them to talk about the world problems, of oil. I want them to watch the presidential debates on TV and talk about that. I want the packed arena, the band playing, cheerleaders, and doing it with kids who are being educated and care about society. I want all that.

And a national championship. [61]

ᏨᎿᎯᏓᎾ

On how he used his summer vacation to prepare for the next season:

I go down to Atlantic Beach for a couple of weeks [in July] with the family and read. I'm an avid reader. The whole month of July I don't do any speaking engagements. I just read. I read just one topic. Three years ago I read about Watergate. Last year I read only humor. . . . After I read and relax I get what I call "the broadstrokes" of next year's team. I don't talk to my assistants. I just think about style, starters, subs, offense, defense, and so on. I always keep my little pad of paper handy and jot down things as they come to me. I try to get away from the everyday nuts and bolts of basketball. Then when I come back from the beach—I come back really excited. [62]

On handling burnout:

I don't know how to guard against burnout. I think certain people are conducive to burnout and others aren't. I mean quite possibly a Tom Landry won't suffer burnout where a Dick Vermeil would. Personality and makeup are the difference. I put myself in the category of Vermeil, unfortunately. I'm aware of the pressures and what's going on. For example, right after we won it [the 1983 national title], I got sick with the flu and took eight days off. There were a lot of things I missed in the enjoyment of sixteen years' work, and I'm going to miss some more time, probably about two weeks, following my hernia operation. [63]

On being the son of a basketball coach, Rocco Valvano:

The positive side was that after the game we'd go back home and really analyze what happened. I'd be able to see the game from the coach's side, as opposed to the player's view. The negative side was that I probably should have been going to a pizza joint with the guys and talking about other things. I was always talking and living basketball. But that was my choice. Dad never forced anything on me. I really had a love affair with the game from an early age. [64]

∞∞∞

On the American Dream:

I happen to be very much a believer in the American Dream. I'm a second-generation Italian kid. My grandfather came over and landed on Ellis Island and the whole thing, and I thought the greatest thing about this country was that you can make it. That's what I tell my kids, that's what I tell my players. If you can build a better mousetrap, do it. If you can write the great American novel, do it. [65]

∞∞∞

On his assessment of 1983 title-game foe Houston after watching the Cougars knock off Louisville in a semifinal game filled with above-the-rim acrobatics:

They were absolutely awesome. I missed the first half, and now I wish I had missed the second. I've never seen anything like that in sixteen years of coaching. I've seen spurts and I've seen streaks, but I've never seen that many different ways to dunk the ball. I gave them some sixes, some sevens on some of their dunks, and I gave [Clyde] Drexler a ten-plus on one of his. It was incredible, and he was actually able to explain it. He had practiced it. [66]

∞∞∞

On his team's strategy going into the 1983 national-champion-ship game against highly favored Houston:

Houston [had] lost to Virginia early in the season, a Virginia without [Ralph] Sampson. Our decisions were fairly simple. We would set the tempo: When we wanted to run, we would run; if we wanted to slow down, we'd do that, too. We never wanted Houston to get out on the break. Another part of our plan was not to allow any dunks, practically the raison d'etre of the Phi Slamma Jammas. We were going with the three-guard offense to draw them away from the basket. We wanted to get Akeem [Olajuwon] in foul trouble. We had to shoot well. And the game had to be in the fifties for us to have a chance to win. [67]

<hr>

On his running around trying to find someone to hug moments after N.C. State had finished off Houston, 54–52, in the 1983 national-title game:

So I ran left, looking for somebody else to hug. Everybody was hugging somebody else. I ran right, looking. Everybody was hugging. There was nobody left to hug! I had just won it all: history, twenty-eighth coach [to win an NCAA title], sixty million watching—and I had nobody to hug! Where was I running? I finally found my athletic director, Willis Casey, my boss, a bit old and out of shape but a very nice man. He gave me my break. He grabbed me. He hugged me. Wonderful! Great! Finally, a hug! . . . Slo-mo. "Chariots of Fire" hug. And then Willis Casey kissed me square on the mouth!

   I had just won the national championship, twenty-eighth

all-time to do it . . . sixty million have watched me running around like a maniac . . . and then I fell into the arms of a sixty-five-year-old, out-of-shape old man who kissed me square on the mouth! The guy watching in Dubuque must have thrown down his beer and said: "Mabel, come look at this." I felt the Thrill of Victory and the Agony of Defeat all at the same time. [68]

ᘓᕬᕮᕬᕢ

On what he told his team on the eve of the 1983 national-title game against Houston:

Whether we win or lose, I told my guys they've carried me on a trip I'll never forget. I thanked them for it. This is a coach's dream. [69]

ᘓᕬᕮᕬᕢ

On his reaction to N.C. State's upset of Houston, yelling outside the arena after it had started to sink in a little later that night:

Phi Slamma Jamma! Phi Slamma Jamma! Tell me about that jive now. [70]

ᘓᕬᕮᕬᕢ

On his being a celebrity:

I set out very calculatedly to become known so that might help me in doing what I had to do. The only thing that I maybe miscalculated was just how easy that would be. For me it was a very natural thing. I like the people. I like to talk to people. Before you know it, I had created a whole other world out there, a whole other business world. [71]

⚭

On the relationship between hard work and success:

It took me ten years to understand the relationship between work and success. I thought if you work hard, you succeed. That's wrong. Everyone is working hard. The truth is, if you don't work hard, you won't be successful. If you do, you just improve your chances. Understanding this helps you deal with failure. I'm not saying each one of us has the world in his hands. There is going to be a lot of failure. But failure is essential to success. [72]

⚭

On his formula for a successful life:

If you can accept the idea that with motivation, dreams, enthusiasm, and hard work, ordinary people can do extraordinary things, I think you're on the way to success. Then the key becomes how to live your life each day. I told everyone that my life had been filled with laughter, with thought, and with emotion. Simply stated, at the end of each day, you should attempt to laugh, to think, and to cry. [73]

⚭

On critics who decry his doing so many things related to making money:

I've done fifteen clinics in parking lots for kids, and I'm the state chairman for six charities. I did it when we were going 14-13, and I'm doing it when we're national champions. And I'll keep doing it because it's fun. There are a lot of things in life more important than basketball. Don't start thinking that all of this is new because I haven't been sitting on my duff for seventeen years. I'm enthusiastic, and I won't ever stop being that way. That all of this stuff ever became fodder for editorials is silly. [74]

On being the host of his own radio show:

I even started calling people to get them to talk to me. Called [Maryland's] Lefty Driesell one night and South Carolina's Bill Foster another night. I asked Lefty to tell everybody what a great radio show I had down here, and Lefty said, "Y'all tune in and listen to the Jim Valvano radio show. It's great." I asked Bill to do the same thing, and he just got on the air and said, "Somebody asked me to talk about the Jim Valvano radio show. I don't even know a Jim Valvano. Never heard of him." [75]

After an 84–83 loss to Virginia:

Lucky for me I have a sense of humor. For eighteen years I built a stockpile of close losses, then the basketball god gave them all back to me at once [in 1983]. Now I'm starting another stockpile. [76]

On his thoughts about dealing with star player Chris Washburn's problems related to his stealing a stereo in a dorm room and struggling academically:

I have fun dealing with the actual coaching of the team. What hasn't been fun has been the explanations of everything. That really gets old. And the Chris Washburn thing has been very distressing to me on a personal, not a basketball, level. [77]

∽∾

On how ACC games rate compared to the NCAA Tournament:

The name of the game is the NCAA and getting a bid to the tournament. That's our major goal, and then you backtrack from there. The regular season is not top priority to us. Sure, you can put a banner up in your gym, but no one really recognizes it. You're just a self-proclaimed champion, that's all. The ACC Tournament winner is the official champion. It's that simple. [78]

∽∾

On the brutality of coaching in the highly competitive Atlantic Coast Conference:

Every time I hear Al McGuire say to Billy Packer on TV, "Don't give me that league stuff," I want to call him [McGuire] up right then. He's never coached in a league like this. He went eleven years at Marquette playing the Sisters of the Poor. We won twenty-nine games last year [at Iona] and we beat the Kansases. But we could also pick and choose when to get up. Here, we play well and lose to Virginia, and I still have to get on their butts and tell them to work harder. And then we go to Carolina and we have to entertain the thought that we might lose there, too. [79]

∞

On reports that his outside interests, to include authoring a cookbook, were distracting him from his coaching duties:

Nobody knows my job like I do. If you want to know how much time I spend coaching basketball, just ask me. Do you really believe I would take time away from my basketball responsibilities to write a cookbook? That I'd say, "Hold up practice, guys, while I finish this last recipe"? Geez. [80]

∞

On his New York roots:

That's still who I am. I don't think I've ever lost sight of who I am. I'm forty. Midlife crisis is supposed to be coming soon—sometime in the next ten years. I guess I'm supposed to grow up. [81]

∞

On life after he left basketball coach to become a TV college basketball analyst:

I've gone to museums. To Broadway shows. On a cruise. I've

met a whole bunch of folks who don't know the difference between a pick and a roll. I've gained ten pounds, but I'm healthy again. With my newfound time to watch late-night TV, I've become hooked on the Home Shopping Network. I've ordered every gadget imaginable, including my new Snack-Master, at which I've become very handy. My family got worried when I started to order the vacuum cleaner attachment that also cuts hair. [Daughter] Jamie said, "We'd better get him out of the house soon."[82]

❦

On his belief that fame and success didn't change him:

I'm absolutely no different than B.C. I call it B.C. and A.C.—Before Championship and After Championship. I'm not doing anything different. They just started noticing me. What interests me is how the people's perspective has changed.[83]

❦

On skeptics who said he couldn't be both head basketball coach and athletic director at N.C. State, a dual role he assumed in February 1986:

How do football coaches be athletic directors? Vince Dooley [at Georgia] has been athletic director for twenty years. Is there something intrinsic about a football coach that allows him to do that, that a basketball coach couldn't do? I think I can do both for a time.

❦

It's the second round of the 1989 NCAAs and Valvano goes airborne to signal a play during the Wolfpack's double-overtime, 102–96 victory over Iowa. (Bob Child photo for AP/Wide World Photos)

On his last public appearance at N.C. State's Reynolds Coliseum in February 1993, speaking during a pregame ceremony honoring the tenth anniversary of his national-championship season:

Nobody had more fun that I did for the ten years [that he was N.C. State coach]. I was fortunate enough to stand in that corner before every game, and thank God for the opportunity to coach at North Carolina State University. . . . This cancer that I have has limited me physically. I can't run and yell at referee John Moreau like I want to. I can't do back flips with our world-class cheerleaders. But this cancer can't touch my mind, my heart, my soul. I will never give up.

❧

Valvano on how to live life:

There are three things we all should do every day, every day of our lives. Number one is laugh. You should laugh every day. Number two is think. Spend some time in thought. And number three, you should have your emotions moved to tears. It could be happiness or joy. But think about it: If you laugh, if you think, and if you cry, that's a full day. That's a heck of a day. You do that seven days a week, and you're going to have something special. [84]

❧

Valvano on continuing to sign autographs for eager fans even while in tremendous physical pain from his cancer and unable to hold a regular pen in hand:

Sometimes it's burdensome. Sometimes I don't feel that good. But I always felt afterward that it's a special role I've been given. It's for all the people who are struggling, dying, fighting it, and trying to have a miracle happen. [85]

⌒⫘⌒

Valvano on looking at the variety of wigs available when contemplating what to wear after he started chemotherapy treatments, even though, ultimately, his hair never did fall out from the treatments:

One of the wigs had hair down to the shoulders, like a rock star's. One was a crew cut, another one had a ponytail, another one made me look like the Beatles. I thought, *God, wouldn't it be great? People could turn on their TVs one night and I'd be Steven Seagal, with the ponytail. The next night they'd turn it on and I'd be a Marine sergeant. The next I'd be a rocker, and the night after that, I wouldn't wear one at all and be Sigourney Weaver in* Alien 3. . . . [86]

⌒⫘⌒

Valvano on how cancer forced him to face the reality of his mortality:

I can't do it, I can't separate from myself anymore. [87]

⌒⫘⌒

Valvano, when sick with cancer, on looking back over his life and the choices he had made:

I can't sit here and swear I'd do everything differently. I wouldn't trade those years. Nobody had more fun than me. How many people do you know who've had their dream come true? You're looking at one. That was my creative period, my run, my burst of energy. [88]

❧

Valvano on his reputation as a coach who put basketball and victories ahead of academics:

Maybe I trusted the kids too much. The school wanted me to force education down their throats, and I wouldn't do it. They wanted me to say, "You don't go to class, you don't play. I take away ball." What does that tell a kid? That ball is more important than education! My approach was, "If you don't study, you pay the consequences. You flunk out. I tried to excite them about learning. I had Dereck Whittenburg read *King Lear* and then go to the chalkboard and do a pre-game talk on it. I wasn't one of those coaches telling them to learn but never read a book myself. I lived it. They saw me reading Shakespeare on buses. They saw me trying things outside of sports all the time. [89]

❧

Valvano on the dearth of funding for cancer research, at least compared to AIDS:

I'm all for AIDS funding and research, but how can the government give ten times as much per AIDS patient as per cancer patient? Barbra Streisand isn't singing for cancer; Elizabeth Taylor isn't holding a celebrity bash for cancer; and yet every time I go into that cancer building at Duke, it's a packed house! If it means more doctors, more space, more money, we've got to get it, because millions of people are going to find out that this is one hell of a way to go. [90]

APPENDIX

Career Game-by-Game Coaching Record

1969-70
Johns Hopkins, 10-9

Haverford	Win	78-49
Gettysburg	Win	70-68
Swarthmore	Win	82-77
Catholic University	Loss	48-66
RPI	Win	76-60
Washington College	Win	71-67
Loyola	Loss	66-77
Penn. Mil. College	Loss	63-67
Western Maryland	Win	72-54
Muhlenberg	Loss	84-86
Towson State	Loss	54-76
Lebanon Valley	Loss	62-79
Drexel	Loss	46-48
Franklin and Marshall	Loss	68-77
Ursinus	Win	64-55
Dickinson	Win	72-64
Loyola	Loss	74-93
Western Maryland	Win	66-61

MAC Tournament

Penn. Mil. College	Loss	61-71

1972-73
Bucknell, 11-14

Chile	Home	Win	86-54
Penn State	Away	Loss	48-61
Scranton	Away	Win	81-48
Rider	Home	Win	61-59
Colgate	Home	Win	76-52
Gannon	Erie, PA	Loss	81-87 (OT)
Lafayette	Erie, PA	Loss	72-74
Stetson	Deland, FL	Loss	55-59 (OT)
Saint Peter's	Deland, FL	Win	92-75
Georgia	Away	Loss	80-97
Georgia Southern	Away	Win	68-63
Armstrong State	Away	Loss	67-70
Pittsburgh	Home	Loss	56-78
Colgate	Away	Loss	56-60
Syracuse	Home	Loss	58-83
Lehigh	Away	Win	75-40
Lafayette	Home	Loss	52-86
Delaware	Home	Loss	83-91 (2-OT)
Rutgers	Home	Loss	69-80
Gettysburg	Away	Loss	66-70
Rider	Away	Win	57-49
Lehigh	Home	Win	70-59
Lafayette	Away	Win	51-49
Delaware	Away	Win	51-49
Gettysburg	Home	Loss	58-60
Dickinson	Away	Win	61-54

1973-74
Bucknell 8-16

Penn State	Home	Loss	57-70
Scranton	Home	Win	86-63
Rider	Away	Loss	48-50
Colgate	Away	Loss	58-91
Kings Point	Scranton, PA	Win	69-42
Wilkes	Scranton, PA	Loss	62-72
Wake Forest	Away	Loss	56-83
Pittsburgh	Away	Loss	62-73
Rochester	Home	Win	89-74
Drexel	Away	Win	52-49
Juniata	Home	Win	75-67
Colgate	Home	Loss	51-52 (OT)
Syracuse	Away	Loss	53-110
Lehigh	Home	Win	56-55
Lafayette	Home	Loss	49-60
Delaware	Away	Loss	73-101
Rutgers	Away	Loss	69-80
Gettysburg	Home	Loss	57-61
Rider	Home	Win	87-60
Lehigh	Away	Loss	56-61
Lafayette	Away	Loss	79-83
Dickinson	Home	Win	68-53
Delaware	Home	Loss	63-77
Gettysburg	Away	Loss	64-78

1974-75
Bucknell, 14-12

South Carolina	Away	Loss	74-88
Bloomsburg	Home	Loss	53-71
Rider	Home	Loss	75-79
Penn State	Home	Loss	83-88 (OT)
Saint Francis	Salem, VA	Loss	68-69
Gettysburg	Salem, VA	Win	83-52
Seton Hall	Away	Loss	61-72
Rochester	Away	Win	105-64
Colgate	Away	Win	73-59
Pittsburgh	Home	Win	72-66
Cornell	Away	Win	78-63
Saint Francis	Home	Win	71-63
Juniata	Away	Win	67-45
Drexel	Home	Win	68-54
Dickinson	Away	Win	80-68
Lehigh	Away	Win	82-62
Rutgers	Home	Loss	72-94
Delaware	Away	Win	63-62
Gettysburg	Away	Win	88-68
Rider	Away	Loss	68-85
Lehigh	Home	Win	74-64
Lafayette	Home	Win	79-65
Delaware	Home	Loss	76-82
Gettysburg	Home	Loss	59-71
Lafayette	Away	Loss	64-96
LaSalle	Away	Loss	74-85

1975-76
Iona, 11-15

Marist	Away	Win	77-74
Siena	Home	Loss	68-75
Columbia	Away	Win	75-73 (OT)
Holy Cross	Away	Loss	80-89
Wagner	Away	Win	76-66
Buffalo	Away	Loss	76-85
Niagara	Away	Loss	58-76
Pace	Home	Win	97-63
Fordham	Home	Win	74-65
Hofstra	Home	Loss	74-75
William & Mary	Home	Win	67-64 (OT)
Fairleigh Dickinson	Home	Win	69-60
Long Island	Away	Win	66-64
Saint Francis (NY)	Away	Loss	62-66
Detroit	Home	Loss	81-85
Rider	Away	Loss	58-66
Massachusetts	Away	Loss	72-88
Maine	Home	Win	84-67
Bridgeport	Home	Win	71-60
Saint Peter's	Away	Loss	73-84
Drexel	Away	Loss	62-67
Army	Home	Win	78-67
LeMoyne	Away	Loss	88-89
Fairfield	Away	Loss	62-87
Seton Hall	Home	Loss	78-79 (OT)
Georgetown	Home	Loss	68-76

1976-77
Iona, 15-10

Marist	Home	Win	106-78
Saint Lawrence	Home	Win	103-95
Siena	Away	Loss	87-95 (OT)
Columbia	Home	Win	84-69
Wagner	Home	Win	77-75
Seton Hall	Away	Loss	83-95
Holy Cross	Home	Loss	79-95
Saint Francis (PA)	Away	Loss	62-88
Fairleigh Dickinson	Away	Loss	62-64
Niagara	Home	Win	71-62
Saint John's	Home	Win	68-66
Detroit	Away	Loss	67-92
Georgetown	Away	Loss	67-81
Rider	Home	Win	83-63
Maine	Away	Win	68-67
Hofstra	Away	Loss	68-80
Fairfield	Home	Win	92-87
Saint Francis (NY)	Home	Win	102-84
Saint Peter's	Away	Loss	70-87
Catholic	Away	Win	89-69
Drexel	Home	Win	69-62
Bridgeport	Away	Win	81-70
Army	Away	Loss	56-62
South Florida	MSG	Win	107-100
Long Island	Home	Win	117-90

(MSG = Madison Square Garden)

1977-78
Iona, 17-10

Saint Lawrence	Home	Win	90-81
Siena	Home	Win	90-83
N. Alabama	Lakeland, FL	Win	69-67
Fla. Southern	Lakeland, FL	Win	51-44
Buffalo	Home	Win	109-79
Holy Cross	Home	Loss	83-105
CCNY	Home	Win	92-76
Auburn	Home	Win	105-82
Kentucky	Away	Loss	65-104
Fairleigh Dickinson	Home	Win	78-61
Saint Bonaventure	Away	Loss	85-93
Pace	Away	Win	110-78
Detroit	Home	Loss	79-84
Niagara	Away	Loss	81-82
East Carolina	Away	Win	96-74
North Carolina State	Away	Loss	72-99
Fairfield	Away	Loss	76-78
Saint Francis (PA)	Home	Win	86-72
Long Island	Away	Win	99-78
Catholic	Home	Win	77-73
Wisconsin-Milwaukee	Home	Win	81-68
Army	Home	Loss	61-63
Centenary	Away	Win	93-83
Saint Peter's	Home	Win	70-57
Saint Francis (NY)	Away	Loss	72-73 (OT)
Wagner	Away	Win	96-83

ECAC Tournament

Saint John's	Uniondale, NY	Loss	80-83

1978-79

Iona, 23-6

Saint Lawrence	Home	Win	107-77
Pace	Home	Win	113-64
Utah State	Syracuse, NY	Win	73-61
Syracuse	Away	Loss	76-89
Fairleigh Dickinson	Away	Win	81-63
Auburn	Away	Loss	66-74
Detroit	MSG	Loss	72-76
New Orleans	Home	Win	75-52
Northeastern	Home	Win	103-88
Saint Mary's (CA)	Home	Win	84-74
East Carolina	Home	Loss	75-76
Wagner	Home	Win	82-78
Niagara	Home	Win	78-66
Wisconsin-Milwaukee	Away	Win	88-75
Saint Peter's	Away	Win	70-68
Alabama-Birm.	Home	Win	61-59
Pittsburgh	Uniondale, NY	Win	84-79 (OT)
Fairfield	Home	Win	97-89
Nevada-Las Vegas	Away	Loss	79-86
Saint Francis (NY)	Home	Win	91-70
Holy Cross	MSG	Win	64-62
Saint Francis (PA)	Away	Win	65-63
Army	Away	Win	55-53
Long Island	Home	Win	81-63
Siena	Away	Win	70-68
Fordham	Home	Win	79-70
ECAC Tournament			
Seton Hall	Uniondale, NY	Win	80-73
Saint John's	Uniondale, NY	Win	63-57
NCAA Tournament			
Pennsylvania	Raleigh, NC	Loss	69-73

1979-80
Iona, 29-5

Texas A&M	Anchorage, AK	Win	78-62
Long Beach State	Anchorage, AK	Win	85-75
Kentucky	Anchorage, AK	Loss	50-57
Saint Mary's (CA)	Away	Win	79-73
San Francisco	Away	Loss	66-78
Fairleigh Dickinson	Home	Win	75-58
Belmont Abbey	Home	Win	54-48
Air Force	Home	Win	64-51
Saint Bonaventure	Home	Win	75-67
Wichita State	Home	Win	84-70
Georgetown	Away	Loss	84-95
Baltimore	Home	Win	68-51
Alabama-Birmingham	Away	Win	70-65
McNeese State	Home	Win	76-66
Niagara	Away	Win	88-74
Pittsburgh	Away	Loss	63-75
Colgate	Home	Win	54-49
Holy Cross	Away	Win	82-67
Wagner	Away	Win	77-73
Fordham	Away	Win	65-59
Saint Peter's	Home	Win	65-62
Kansas	MSG	Win	81-77
Army	Home	Win	67-54
Saint Francis (NY)	Home	Win	72-62
Manhattan	Away	Win	70-57
Long Island	Away	Win	85-72
Siena	Home	Win	84-72
Louisville	MSG	Win	77-60
Fairfield	Away	Win	74-53

ECAC Tournament

Fairleigh Dickinson	Home	Win	69-53
Siena	Jamaica, NY	Win	76-70
Saint Peter's	Jamaica, NY	Win	64-46

NCAA Tournament

Holy Cross	Providence, RI	Win	84-78
Georgetown	Providence, RI	Loss	71-74

221

1980-81
North Carolina State, 14-13

North Carolina-			
Wilmington	Home	Win	83-59
Davidson	Home	Win	89-72
Wake Forest	Greensboro, NC	Loss	57-87
Duke	Greensboro, NC	Win	74-60
Campbell	Home	Win	82-56
Appalachian State	Home	Win	71-47
Maryland	Away	Loss	75-82
Iona	New York	Win	61-58
Saint John's	New York	Win	64-55
Clemson	Away	Loss	68-76
Virginia	Away	Loss	55-63
Georgia Tech	Home	Win	93-68
North Carolina	Away	Loss	70-73
Wake Forest	Away	Loss	52-60
Duke	Home	Loss	47-56
East Carolina	Home	Win	77-52
Georgia Tech	Away	Win	70-55
North Carolina	Home	Loss	54-57
Clemson	Home	Loss	76-82
Furman	Charlotte, NC	Win	77-60
Saint Joseph's	Charlotte, NC	Win	47-42
Virginia	Home	Loss	46-51
Notre Dame	Home	Loss	55-71
Duke	Away	Win	52-51
Maryland	Home	Loss	72-76
Wake Forest	Home	Win	66-65

ACC Tournament

North Carolina	Landover, MD	Loss	54-69

1981-82
North Carolina State, 22-10

Campbell	Home	Win	68-53
Davidson	Charlotte, NC	Win	76-55
Saint Francis (PA)	Home	Win	89-56
Saint Peter's	Home	Win	44-43
Appalachian State	Home	Win	66-38
Maryland	Home	Win	74-53
N.C.-Wilmington	Home	Win	77-43
Michigan State	Honolulu, HI	Win	67-46
Wichita State	Honolulu, HI	Win	60-48
Rice	Honolulu, HI	Loss	47-51
Clemson	Home	Win	75-59
Southern Mississippi	Home	Win	46-45
Georgia Tech	Away	Win	55-49
North Carolina	Home	Loss	41-61
Wake Forest	Away	Win	52-50
Duke	Away	Loss	48-49
East Carolina	Home	Win	63-53
Georgia Tech	Home	Win	49-40
North Carolina	Away	Loss	44-58
Clemson	Away	Loss	54-65
The Citadel	Charlotte, NC	Win	54-44
Furman	Charlotte, NC	Win	67-55
Virginia	Home	Loss	36-39
Notre Dame	Away	Win	62-42
Duke	Home	Win	72-56
Virginia	Away	Loss	40-45
Loyola (MD)	Home	Win	80-52
Maryland	Away	Loss	38-52
Wake Forest	Home	Loss	46-50

ACC Tournament

Maryland	Greensboro, NC	Win	40-28
North Carolina	Greensboro, NC	Loss	46-58

NCAA Tournament

Tenn.-Chattanooga	Indianapolis, IN	Loss	51-58

1982-83
North Carolina State, 26-10, National Champions

Western Carolina	Home	Win	103-66
North Carolina A&T	Home	Win	100-70
East Carolina	Home	Win	57-49
Michigan State	Home	Win	45-41
Louisville	Away	Loss	52-57
West Virginia	Meadowlands, NJ	Win	67-59
Fairleigh Dickinson	Home	Win	111-76
Clemson	Away	Win	76-70
Missouri	Away	Loss	42-49
Virginia	Home	Loss	80-88
Georgia Tech	Home	Win	81-61
North Carolina	Away	Loss	81-99
Wake Forest	Away	Loss	73-91
Memphis State	Home	Loss	53-57
Duke	Home	Win	94-79
Maryland	Away	Loss	81-86
Georgia Tech	Away	Win	74-64
Furman	Charlotte, NC	Win	51-48
The Citadel	Charlotte, NC	Win	57-47
Clemson	Home	Win	90-83
Notre Dame	Home	Loss	42-43
N.C.-Wilmington	Home	Win	90-69
North Carolina	Home	Win	70-63
Duke	Away	Win	96-79
Virginia	Away	Loss	75-86
Maryland	Home	Loss	58-67
Wake Forest	Home	Win	130-89

ACC Tournament

Wake Forest	Atlanta	Win	71-70
North Carolina	Atlanta	Win	91-84 (OT)
Virginia	Atlanta	Win	81-78

NCAA Tournament

Pepperdine	Corvalis, OR	Win	69-67 (2-OT)
UNLV	Corvalis, OR	Win	71-70
Utah	Ogden, UT	Win	75-56
Virginia	Ogden, UT	Win	63-62
Georgia	Albuquerque, NM	Win	67-60
Houston	Albuquerque, NM	Win	54-52

1983-84
North Carolina State, 19-14

Houston	Springfield, MA	Win	76-64
Alaska-Anchorage	Anchorage, AK	Win	68-60
Santa Clara	Anchorage, AK	Win	78-75
Arkansas	Anchorage, AK	Win	65-60
N.C-Charlotte	Greensboro, NC	Win	79-60
Virginia Tech	Greensboro, NC	Loss	65-89
Western Carolina	Home	Win	82-61
Hofstra	Home	Win	82-56
Louisville	Home	Loss	79-83
North Carolina A&T	Home	Win	84-71
Towson State	Home	Win	88-49
Campbell	Home	Win	80-65
Maryland	Home	Loss	55-59
North Carolina	Home	Loss	60-81
Clemson	Away	Loss	61-63
Virginia	Away	Loss	54-57
Georgia Tech	Away	Loss	47-56
N.C.-Wilmington	Home	Win	81-53
Wake Forest	Home	Win	80-69
Duke	Away	Win	79-76
Missouri	Home	Win	66-53
The Citadel	Charlotte, NC	Win	50-49
Furman	Charlotte, NC	Win	95-72
Clemson	Home	Win	69-59
Georgia Tech	Home	Win	68-67
Northeastern	Home	Win	77-74
North Carolina	Away	Loss	71-95
Duke	Home	Loss	70-73 (OT)
Virginia	Home	Loss	63-74
Maryland	Away	Loss	50-63
Wake Forest	Away	Loss	75-84

ACC Tournament
Maryland	Greensboro, NC	Loss	63-69

National Invitation Tournament
Florida State	Raleigh, NC	Loss	71-74 (OT)

225

1984-85
North Carolina State, 23-10

Campbell	Home	Win	94-54
Cal.-Santa Barbara	Home	Win	93-70
Hartford	Home	Win	83-46
North Carolina A&T	Home	Win	101-54
Western Carolina	Home	Win	103-67
Georgia Tech	Home	Loss	64-66
Saint Francis	Home	Win	82-64
Rutgers	New York	Win	80-68
Saint John's	New York	Loss	56-66
Maryland	Away	Loss	56-58
Kentucky	Away	Loss	62-78
Virginia	Home	Win	51-45
Clemson	Away	Win	71-68
North Carolina	Away	Loss	76-86
Florida State	Home	Win	72-66
Duke	Home	Win	89-71
Louisville	Away	Loss	78-84
Georgia Tech	Away	Win	61-53
Wake Forest	Away	Loss	64-91
Clemson	Home	Win	69-57
SMU	Home	Win	82-78 (OT)
Maryland	Home	Win	90-51
North Carolina	Home	Win	85-76
Duke	Away	Win	70-66
Virginia	Away	Win	57-55
Maryland	Home	Loss	70-71
Wake Forest	Home	Win	66-64

ACC Tournament

Clemson	Atlanta	Win	70-63
North Carolina	Atlanta	Loss	51-57

NCAA Tournament

Nevada-Reno	Albuquerque, NM	Win	65-56
Texas-El Paso	Albuquerque, NM	Win	86-73
Alabama	Denver	Win	61-55
Saint John's	Denver	Loss	60-69

1985-86
North Carolina State, 21-13

Western Carolina	Home	Win	80-57
Furman	Home	Win	94-56
Loyola-Chicago	Away	Loss	58-60
Tampa	Home	Win	88-64
Florida State	Away	Loss	67-76
Kansas	Greensboro, NC	Loss	56-71
Wake Forest	Home	Win	77-64
Radford	Home	Win	92-57
Chaminade	Honolulu, HI	Win	64-46
UNLV	Honolulu, HI	Win	80-73
Monmouth	Home	Win	106-53
North Carolina	Away	Loss	79-80
North Carolina A&T	Home	Win	66-48
Duke	Away	Loss	64-74
Clemson	Home	Win	60-57
Wake Forest	Away	Win	45-44
Maryland	Away	Win	67-55
Virginia	Home	Win	55-53
Georgia Tech	Home	Loss	54-67
Kentucky	Home	Win	54-51
Clemson	Away	Win	73-69 (OT)
Louisville	Home	Win	76-64
Brooklyn College	Home	Win	103-52
Maryland	Home	Loss	66-67
Duke	Home	Loss	70-72
Virginia	Away	Loss	60-69
North Carolina	Home	Win	76-65
Georgia Tech	Away	Loss	57-69
Oklahoma	Away	Loss	69-72

ACC Tournament

Virginia	Greensboro, NC	Loss	62-64

NCAA Tournament

Iowa	Minneapolis, MN	Win	66-64
Arkansas-L.R.	Minneapolis, MN	Win	81-66 (2-OT)
Iowa State	Kansas City, MO	Win	70-66
Kansas	Kansas City, MO	Loss	67-75

1986-87
North Carolina State, 20-15

Navy	Springfield, MA	Win	84-80
Texas	Anchorage, AK	Win	69-68
Iowa	Anchorage, AK	Loss	89-90 (OT)
Utah State	Home	Win	94-82
East Tennessee State	Home	Win	104-85
Western Carolina	Away	Win	96-75
Duquesne	Home	Win	82-59
N.C.-Asheville	Home	Win	81-65
Tampa	Away	Loss	62-67
Loyola-Chicago	Home	Win	97-85
Maryland	Home	Win	69-47
Clemson	Away	Loss	69-73
Georgia Tech	Home	Win	63-62
Wake Forest	Home	Win	75-67
North Carolina	Away	Loss	78-96
Duke	Home	Win	87-74
Kansas	Kansas City	Loss	60-74
Virginia	Away	Loss	60-61
Oklahoma	Home	Loss	82-86
DePaul	Away	Loss	62-84
North Carolina	Home	Loss	79-95
Louisville	Away	Loss	75-87
Winthrop	Home	Win	85-58
Clemson	Home	Loss	75-78
Georgia Tech	Away	Loss	76-87
Brooklyn College	Home	Win	107-79
Duke	Away	Loss	50-65
Virginia	Home	Loss	65-72
Maryland	Away	Win	85-72
Wake Forest	Away	Win	80-76 (OT)
Chicago State	Home	Win	86-78

ACC Tournament

Duke	Landover, MD	Win	71-64 (OT)
Wake Forest	Landover, MD	Win	77-73 (2-OT)
North Carolina	Landover, MD	Win	68-67

NCAA Tournament

Florida	Syracuse, NY	Loss	70-82

1987-88
North Carolina State, 24-8

Vermont	Home	Win	108-58
Tampa	Home	Win	85-60
Kansas	Home	Loss	67-74
Winthrop	Home	Win	93-59
Santa Barbara	Away	Loss	78-96
Creighton	Honolulu, HI	Win	86-55
Louisville	Honolulu, HI	Win	80-75
Arizona State	Honolulu, HI	Win	83-71
Cornell	Home	Win	95-72
Clemson	Home	Win	70-61
Morgan State	Home	Win	103-54
Georgia Tech	Away	Win	76-74
Wake Forest	Away	Loss	67-71
North Carolina	Home	Loss	73-77
Maryland	Away	Win	83-81
DePaul	Home	Win	71-66
Virginia	Home	Win	75-69
Duke	Away	Win	77-74
Baptist	Home	Win	116-68
North Carolina	Away	Loss	73-75 (OT)
Louisville	Home	Win	101-89
Maryland-Balt.	Home	Win	99-77
Clemson	Away	Win	88-63
Georgia Tech	Home	Loss	84-87
Duke	Home	Win	89-78
Virginia	Away	Win	64-63
N.C.-Asheville	Home	Win	87-76
Maryland	Home	Win	74-68
Wake Forest	Home	Win	86-82

ACC Tournament

Clemson	Greensboro, NC	Win	79-71
Duke	Greensboro, NC	Loss	71-73

NCAA Tournament

Murray State	Lincoln, NE	Loss	75-78

1988-89
North Carolina State, 22-9

Columbia	Home	Win	110-54
Akron	Home	Win	87-67
SMU	Away	Loss	57-59
Alabama State	Home	Win	109-81
Coppin State	Home	Win	100-67
Monmouth	Home	Win	95-50
Virginia Mil. Institute	Home	Win	105-79
Towson State	Home	Win	83-77
Clemson	Away	Win	73-65
Temple	Home	Win	71-59
Coastal Carolina	Home	Win	97-69
Georgia Tech	Home	Win	82-68
Wake Forest	Home	Win	82-64
North Carolina	Away	Loss	81-84
Duke	Home	Win	88-73
Maryland	Away	Win	90-67
Virginia	Away	Loss	71-91
DePaul	Away	Loss	74-81
North Carolina	Home	Win	98-88
UNLV	Home	Loss	80-89
Clemson	Home	Win	90-75
Georgia Tech	Away	Win	71-69
N.C.-Asheville	Home	Win	90-75
Duke	Away	Loss	65-86
Virginia	Home	Loss	75-76
Maryland	Home	Win	94-77
Wake Forest	Away	Win	110-103 (4-OT)

ACC Tournament

Maryland	Atlanta	Loss	49-71

NCAA Tournament

South Carolina	Providence, RI	Win	81-66
Iowa	Providence, RI	Win	102-96 (2-OT)
Georgetown	East Rutherford, NJ	Loss	61-69

1989-90
North Carolina State, 18-12

Richmond	Home	Win	57-48
DePaul	Away	Loss	63-70
Appalachian State	Home	Win	97-67
Ohio State	Charlotte, NC	Win	68-54
Pittsburgh	Charlotte, NC	Win	100-87
Saint John's	Greensboro, NC	Win	67-53
Duquesne	Home	Win	126-77
East Tennessee State	Home	Loss	82-92
N.C.-Asheville	Home	Win	110-70
Florida State	New York	Win	90-72
Seton Hall	New York	Win	65-62
Clemson	Home	Win	79-77
Temple	Atlantic City, NJ	Win	74-71
Boston University	Home	Win	95-70
Georgia Tech	Away	Loss	85-92
Wake Forest	Away	Win	61-57
North Carolina	Home	Loss	81-91
Duke	Away	Loss	82-85 (OT)
Maryland	Home	Win	81-61
Virginia	Home	Win	84-58
UNLV	Away	Loss	82-88
North Carolina	Away	Win	88-77
DePaul	Home	Win	80-71
Clemson	Away	Loss	81-89
Georgia Tech	Home	Loss	92-95 (2-OT)
Duke	Home	Win	76-71
Virginia	Away	Loss	71-77
Maryland	Away	Loss	95-96
Wake Forest	Home	Loss	91-93

ACC Tournament

Georgia Tech	Charlotte, NC	Loss	67-76

TOTALS

Johns Hopkins	(1 season)	10-9	(.526)
Bucknell	(3 seasons)	33-42	(.440)
Iona	(5 seasons)	95-46	(.674)
N.C. State	(10 seasons)	209-114	(.647)
Totals	**(19 seasons)**	**347-212**	**(.621)**

NOTES

Chapter 2: N.C. State and the Cardiac Pack

1. Joe Menzer, *Four Corners* (New York: Simon and Schuster, 1999), 229.
2. Gary Smith, "As Times Runs Out," *Sports Illustrated*, January 11, 1993.

Chapter 3: Jimmy V vs. the Big C

1. Gary Smith, "Jimmy Vee Hung in There," *Sports Illustrated*, May 10, 1993.

Chapter 4: The Valvano Legacy

1. Joe Menzer, *Four Corners* (New York: Simon and Schuster, 1999), 240.
2. Gary Smith, "As Times Runs Out," *Sports Illustrated*, January 11, 1993.
3. Menzer, *Four Corners*, 261–62.
4. Ibid., 262.
5. Ibid., 242–243.
6. Ibid., 243.
7. Ibid., 215.
8. Ibid.

Chapter 5: In His Own Words

1. Jim Valvano, with Curry Kirkpatrick, *Valvano: They Gave Me a Lifetime Contract, and Then They Declared Me Dead* (New York: Pocket Books, 1991), 1.
2. North Carolina State basketball brochure, *North Carolina State Basketball: A Championship Tradition*.
3. Ibid.
4. Ibid.
5. Unidentified newspaper clipping.
6. *Sunday News Magazine* (city of origin unknown), February 11, 1979.
7. Valvano and Kirkpatrick, *Lifetime Contract*, 9.
8. Ibid., 31.
9. *Sunday News Magazine*, February 11, 1979.
10. Valvano and Kirkpatrick, *Lifetime Contract*, 106.
11. Ibid., 112.
12. Ibid., 180.
13. *Charlotte Observer*, an undetermined 1980 issue.
14. *Boston Globe* story that appeared in the *Houston Chronicle*, May 31, 1983.
15. *New York Daily News*, December 26, 1980.
16. Associated Press story, *Asheville* (N.C.) *Citizen*, December 24, 1980.
17. *Charlotte Observer*, July 24, 1981.
18. Ibid.
19. Associated Press story, *Asheville Citizen*, December 24, 1980.
20. *Fayetteville Times*, October 23, 1981.
21. Associated Press story, *Asheville Citizen*, December 24, 1980.
22. Ibid.
23. Ibid.
24. *Raleigh News and Observer*, date unknown.
25. *Charlotte Observer*, May 18, 1980.
26. *Greensboro Daily News*, March 28, 1980.
27. *Greensboro Daily News*, date unknown.

NOTES

28. *Charlotte Observer*, November 13, 1981.

29. *Asheville Citizen*, May 14, 1981.

30. *Raleigh News and Observer*, May 17, 1980.

31. *Asheville Times*, May 14, 1981.

32. *Indianapolis News*, date unknown.

33. Valvano and Kirkpatrick, *Lifetime Contract*, 131.

34. *Fayetteville Times*, October 23, 1981.

35. *Durham Sun*, February 25, 1981.

36. *Indianapolis News*, date unknown.

37. *Charlotte Observer*, May 27, 1981.

38. Ibid.

39. *Raleigh News and Observer*, May 17, 1980.

40. *Greensboro News and Record*, November 25, 1987.

41. Ibid.

42. *Boston Globe* story in the *Houston Chronicle*, May 31, 1983.

43. Associated Press story, *Asheville Citizen*, January 8, 1982.

44. *Raleigh News and Observer*, date unknown.

45. *Washington Post*, February 21, 1982.

46. Valvano and Kirkpatrick, *Lifetime Contract*, 187–88.

47. Ibid., 313.

48. *Charlotte Observer*, February 3, 1981.

49. *Salisbury Post*, June 2, 1982.

50. Valvano and Kirkpatrick, *Lifetime Contract*, 39.

51. Ibid., 41.

52. *Salisbury Post*, June 2, 1982.

53. *Greensboro Daily News*, January 30, 1981.

54. Valvano and Kirkpatrick, *Lifetime Contract*, 101.

55. *Raleigh News and Observer*, May 3, 1982.

56. Valvano and Kirkpatrick, *Lifetime Contract*, 298–99.

57. *Spectator*, June 30, 1983.

58. *Raleigh News and Observer*, February 1, 1982.

59. *Washington Post*, February 21, 1982.

60. *Durham Sun*, February 25, 1981.

61. *Raleigh News and Observer*, February 1, 1982.

62. *Spectator*, June 30, 1983.

63. Craig Barnes, "N.C. State's Valvano: Maestro of the Miracle," publication unknown.

64. *Scholastic Coach*, September 1983.

65. *Sport* magazine, date unknown.

66. *Raleigh News and Observer*, April 4, 1983.

67. Valvano and Kirkpatrick, *Lifetime Contract*, 62.

68. Ibid., 167.

69. *Pittsburgh Press*, April 4, 1983.

70. *New York Daily News*, April 6, 1983.

71. New York Times News Service.

72. *Cary* (N.C.) *News*, June 5, 1983.

73. Valvano and Kirkpatrick, *Lifetime Contract*, 170.

74. *Wilmington Star*, October 3, 1983.

75. *Greensboro Daily News and Record*, February 12, 1984.

76. *Greensboro Daily News*, January 14, 1984.

77. *New York Times*, February 15, 1985.

78. *Raleigh News and Observer*, February 15, 1985.

79. *Greensboro Daily News*, January 30, 1981.

80. *Raleigh Times*, February 14, 1985.

81. *New York Post*, February 21, 1986.

82. Valvano and Kirkpatrick, *Lifetime Contract*, 321.

83. *The Sporting News*, February 11, 1985.

84. Menzer, *Four Corners*, 259.

85. Menzer, *Four Corners*, 261.

86. Gary Smith, "Jimmy Vee Hung in There," *Sports Illustrated*, May 10, 1993.

87. Gary Smith, "As Times Runs Out," *Sports Illustrated*, January 11, 1993.

88. Ibid.

89. Ibid.

90. Ibid.

INDEX

CPSIA information can be obtained
at www.ICGtesting.com
Printed in the USA
BVOW05*2156281216
472075BV00034B/445/P

9 781581 822199